Excel Form
That Automate Tasks
You No Longer Have
Time For

Plus Bonus Chapters:

- **Excel Pivot Tables That Automate Tasks**
- **Excel Macros That Automatically Send Emails**

Erik Kopp

ISBN-13: 978-1534648715
ISBN-10: 1534648712

Has This Happened To You?

Your organization has "restructured" and now you have several times the amount of work to do by yourself and not much time in which to get it done, and no excuses for errors. The requests for information, analyses and reports keep pouring in non-stop and the deadlines are all just around the corner because everything is "urgent". Getting more help, more time or reducing the workload are all out of the question - so to survive you really need to make every second count and get as much done as you possibly can in the very least amount of time, because time is money and you don't have a lot of either.

Before you stress-out and totally panic, think about how you might be better able to get your information management work done using the resources which you do have. While many organizations have cut way back on manual resources (people), very few if any have cut back on electronic resources and infrastructure (computers, software and networks). In fact most businesses have invested in these areas because they want their remaining people to have the most up to date computers and systems to enable them to be more productive.

So what can these computers do for you? They can perform many of the more repetitive and tedious information management tasks which can take up lots and lots of valuable time if performed manually. A standard MS Office Computer can do a lot more than just email, word processing, and presentations. Excel contains some very valuable functions which enable you to quickly and accurately analyze and manipulate information as well as transform and present it. With a little knowledge of how to set these function up, you can analyze 10,000 pieces of data and provide answers to complex questions in just seconds. This also means that when the people asking the question invariable come back with more what-if questions, you can reanalyze the information just as quickly.

What follows are real life examples of situations that occur commonly in many business and personal situations where you need to manage large sets of data to produce valuable information which meets someone's requirements. The examples shown use Excel 2007.

TABLE OF CONTENTS

The Amazing Tools At Your Disposal Can Save The Day

One of the most valuable data management tools commonly available to many people is MS Excel. This powerful software can not only be used for presenting information in tables, charts and graphs, and doing calculations but it also has many powerful database functions which I will describe in detail in a little bit.

Some people think this stuff is really cool, but I know some of you are hesitant to try this because it sounds like "programming" and programming is complicated, hard to understand and just plain boring. But unlike software coding, Excel is set up to be very logical and intuitive, so that more people will buy it and use it.

Before we even get to Excel let's define what is meant by automating a task and how to identify what tasks can and should be automated. Computers are very good at consistently following instructions exactly as written. Therefore if you have an information management task where:

- The data is available in electronic format (can be plain text outside of Excel – we'll discuss that later)

- The task can be clearly and consistently defined (Example: Every item over $5.00 gets marked down 10% for the next 5 days and identified as a "SALE" item, every item over $20.00 gets marked down 15% for the next 2 days and identified as a "CLEARANCE" item).

- The task is very repetitive and would take you more than 15 minutes to do manually (a list of 10 items might be faster to do manually, but a list of 1,000 items is worth automating).

- There is a high risk of inaccuracies (if you make a mistake it will cost the company or you so you need to check your results to ensure they make sense in all cases).

If you have identified a task which meets these criteria above, this is definitely a candidate for automation. The time spent up front setting up the functions will be well worth the effort in the long run.

So now that you have identified the task you need help with, how do you go about "automating this"? This is starting to sound like programming....but let's not panic and look at this very logically. Instead of thinking in terms of writing a program, think about how you would solve this yourself if you performed the task manually. If you need a visual cue, use the outline below and fill in the details as needed.

Here is a stepwise outline to assist in automating as repetitive task:

Name of Task:_____

1. **What is the data I have?_____**
2. **What is the result I need?_____**
3. **What would I do with the data first to get to the result?_____**
4. **What would I do with the data next to get to the result?_____**
5. **What would I do with the data next to get to the result?_____**
6. **.....**

7. **How would I check that the results are correct?_____**

Let's say you have inventory and pricing data in a retail setting and you need to identify your sale items based on the criteria noted above (Every item over $5.00 gets marked down 10% for the next 5 days and identified as a "SALE" item, every item over $20.00 gets marked down 15% for the next 2 days and identified as a "CLEARANCE" item).

For this example, your outline will look like this –

Name of Task: Identify Sale and Clearance Items.

1. **What is the data I have? Inventory and Price List.**

2. **What is the result I need? List of Items on Sale (Item ID, Name, Adjusted Price, Sale End Date).**

3. **What would I do with the data first to get to the result? Get the list into a table.**

4. **What would I do with the data next to get to the result? Find any price greater than 5.00 but not more than 20.00 and identify it as a SALE item.**

5. **What would I do with the data next to get to the result? Find any price above 20.00 and identify it as a CLEARANCE item.**

6. **What would I do with the data next to get to the result? Assign an adjusted price equal to current price x 0.9 for SALE items.**

7. **What would I do with the data next to get to the result? Assign an adjusted price equal to current price x 0.85 for CLEARANCE items.**

8. What would I do with the data next to get to the result? <u>Assign an end date of today's date + 5 for SALE items</u>.

9. What would I do with the data next to get to the result? <u>Assign an end date of today's date + 2 for CLEARANCE items</u>.

10. What would I do with the data next to get to the result? <u>Consolidate a list of all SALE items (Item ID, Name, Adjusted Price, Sale End Date)</u>.

11. What would I do with the data next to get to the result? <u>Consolidate a list of all CLEARANCE items (Item ID, Name, Sale Price, Sale End Date)</u>.

12. How would I check that the results are correct? <u>For each SALE Item, ensure the original price is the adjusted price + 10% and it is greater than 5.00 but less than 20.00.</u>

13. How would I check that the results are correct? <u>For each CLEARANCE Item, ensure the original price is the sale price + 15% and it is greater than 20.00.</u>

14. How would I check that the results are correct? <u>Ensure the sale end date – today's date is equal to 5 for SALE items and equal to 2 for CLEARANCE items.</u>

15. How would I check that the results are correct? <u>Ensure there are no other items on the list greater than 5.00 and less than 20.00 or greater than 20.00 which are not identified and assigned adjusted prices.</u>

Wow! This sounds like a whole lot of work and not time savings. But just think about it, if you were doing this manually or you were showing someone else how to do this wouldn't you be following these same steps – even if you did not write this down?

So this is the first step to figuring out what needs to be done, whether you do it manually or automate it. The steps that need to be performed are the same, the only difference is whether a person does it or a computer does it.

Looking at the criteria above, we said if this is a task you can perform yourself in 15 minutes or less and you only have to do it once, then do it yourself and get it done.

But if this is long list (500 items or 5,000 items or 10,000 items..) or if you think you will need to do this same thing over and again for different lists or at different times, then it would be wise to automate this task.

The next steps would then be to go back over this outline and set up Excel to perform each of these steps using a function. Once this is set up, it can be applied to as many pieces of data as you have and used as many times as you need to use it.

This is very handy when speed and accuracy count and it also is a great help when there are typically multiple ongoing requests. Let's say your boss looks at your report you generated using the logic above and then asks "What is the total reduction in profits resulting from the Sales this week?", and then they ask "What if we only reduced Clearance Items by 12% instead of 15%, then what would be the reduction in profits?"…."What if SALES ended in 4 days instead of 5, then what would be the reduction in profits?"…..

If you had to go back and recalculate all of this manually each time, this would be extremely time consuming and also very aggravating. And you know your boss is going to ask, so the time invested in automating this up front is well worth the effort.

So these are the steps to follow for any repetitive tedious information management tasks you need to do. Think about it as being very logical (and not as programming) and being very efficient and smart if getting the most work done in the least time. Put the computers to work, let them do the time consuming mindless stuff for you. You will see your productivity, your value and your outlook on life improve.

What follows are real life detailed examples of repetitive time consuming data management tasks which have been automated using Excel functions following this logical approach. I am not a programmer and do not know the first thing about coding, but this is very logical and easy to follow.

Give it a try – you have nothing to lose!

How To Instantly Create A Spreadsheet Listing Files In Any Drive Or Folder

TASK – <u>Identify all of the 300+ files you have received on a USB drive and provide a complete list to your boss.</u>

How to do this? You could either use –

Option A – Open the folder on the drive and print the screen, then scroll down, print the screen… and then copy down all the file IDs to a Text file or Excel.   This will take several hundred steps and several hours to complete.   You may miss some or make some mistakes along the way, so you will need to double-check your work, so allow another hour or so.

Or

Option B – Let The Computer Do The Work.

This is a basic operating system function for a computer to be able to create a file listing the directory of files. Back in the old days of DOS, this was a very routine task for us old time computer geeks. But now in the days of graphical interfaces and flashy apps, this is not as apparent. Windows will show you what's inside a folder, but the screen only shows you 50 or so files and then you need to scroll down. If you want to make a text file or spreadsheet listing the file names, you cannot copy and paste these.

So here is what you do.

Open the command prompt Window by clicking **Start->Run**

And then enter "cmd", click "OK"

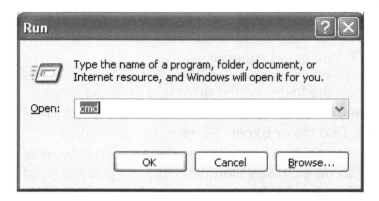

Change the default directory (the old name for Folder) to be what you are looking for by typing "**cd /D X:\Folder\SubFolder**", where "X" is the drive letter and Folder is the first level folder and SubFolder is the next, etc until you have the complete path to the files you are looking for.

Once the prompt shows the folder you are interested in cataloging, then type "**dir/b/s>dirlist.txt**"

This will create a file called "dirlist.txt" which will contain a listing of all the files in the folder you are looking at. You can modify the directory listing using the command line switches shown below.

/B Uses bare format (no heading information or summary)
/L Forces lowercase display of file names
/O List by files in sorted order:
      N by name (alphabetical)
      S by size (smallest first)
      E by extension (alphabetical)

D by date/time (oldest first)
G group directories first
- using this prefix reverses the sort order
/P Pauses after each screen of information
/S Lists files in the specified directory and all subdirectories
/W Uses wide list format
/X Displays 8.3 versions of long file names
/? Displays a full list of command line switches

For this example, let's continue with the command as shown above and look at this folder shown below.

To make a list of this using Windows is very tedious to scroll down and capture all the files names. But using the command above will give us a quick list in seconds.

Once we have the text list, we can open this in Excel and sort it, fix it up and make it look pretty before presenting it to our boss.

So here we go -

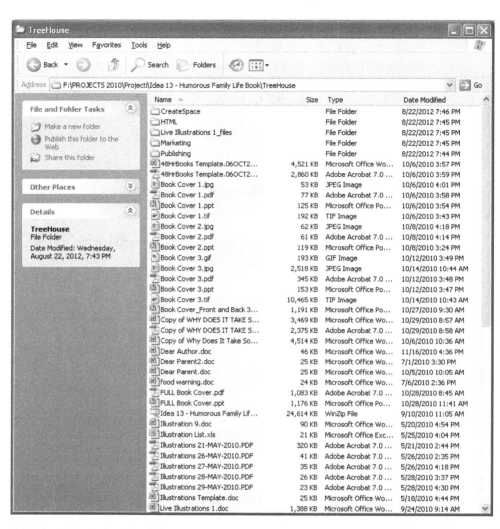

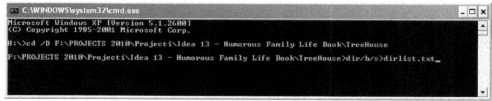

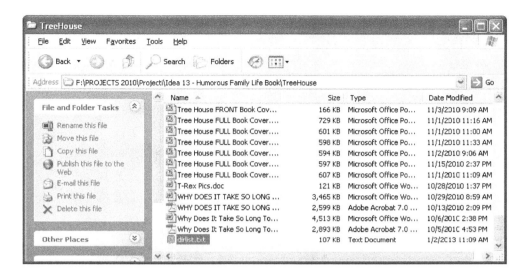

Here is the Text file generated. Notice it shows all subfolders and folder trees as well.

This list can be opened with Excel and displayed and sorted as needed.

To do this, select the "dirlist.txt" file, right-click and select "Open With" and select "Microsoft Office Excel" from the list of applications -

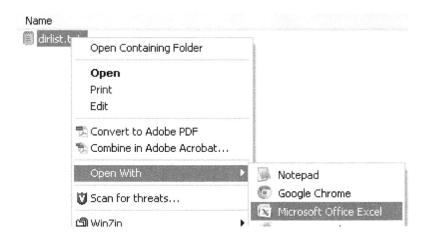

When the list opens in Excel, you will see all the rows containing the files names and paths. If you need to break this down or sort it, first highlight Column A (click on the "A")

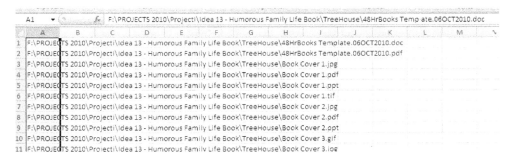

Then select "Data" "Text To Columns" –

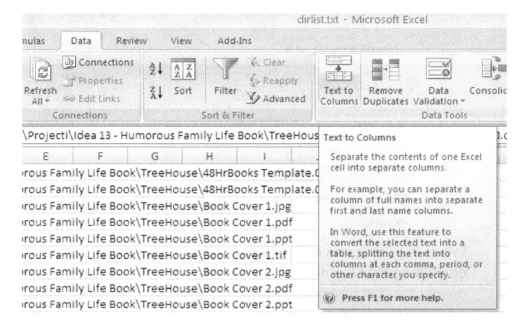

This will open the Convert Text to Columns Wizard.

From this window (Step 1 of 3), select "Delimited" for your data. This means that all the fields in the data are separated by a specific separator character. In this case the path, subfolder, file name are separated by the character "\".

Then click "Next".

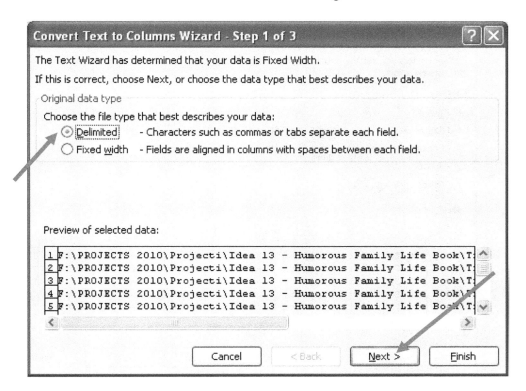

This will open the next window (Step 2 of 3). In this window, select the Delimiter as "Other" and type in the character "\". The window will then show you a preview of how the data will be separated. Then click "Next" –

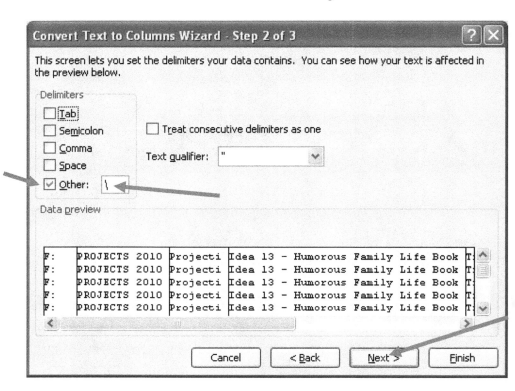

The next window (Step 3) allows you to change the data format to text, date, numeric, general etc. General will automatically convert the data to the appropriate format as determined by the contents of the cells. The default is General and this works for this data, so just click "Finish" -

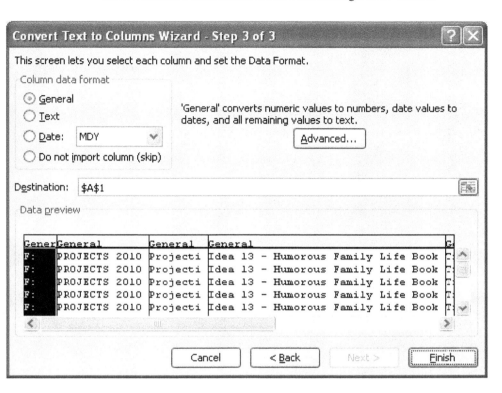

And you are done - Excel will now show you the data in a spreadsheet format with the drive, folders, subfolders and file names in their own columns.

DRIVE	FOLDER	SubFolder1	SubFolder2	SubFolder3	File Name	File Type
F	PROJECTS 2010	Project1	Idea 13 - Humorous Family Life Book	TreeHouse	48HrBooks Template_06OCT2010.doc	doc
F	PROJECTS 2010	Project1	Idea 13 - Humorous Family Life Book	TreeHouse	48HrBooks Template_06OCT2010.pdf	pdf
F	PROJECTS 2010	Project1	Idea 13 - Humorous Family Life Book	TreeHouse	Book Cover 1.jpg	jpg
F	PROJECTS 2010	Project1	Idea 13 - Humorous Family Life Book	TreeHouse	Book Cover 1.pdf	pdf
F	PROJECTS 2010	Project1	Idea 13 - Humorous Family Life Book	TreeHouse	Book Cover 1.ppt	ppt
F	PROJECTS 2010	Project1	Idea 13 - Humorous Family Life Book	TreeHouse	Book Cover 1.tif	tif
F	PROJECTS 2010	Project1	Idea 13 - Humorous Family Life Book	TreeHouse	Book Cover 2.jpg	jpg
F	PROJECTS 2010	Project1	Idea 13 - Humorous Family Life Book	TreeHouse	Book Cover 2.pdf	pdf
F	PROJECTS 2010	Project1	Idea 13 - Humorous Family Life Book	TreeHouse	Book Cover 2.ppt	ppt
F	PROJECTS 2010	Project1	Idea 13 - Humorous Family Life Book	TreeHouse	Book Cover 3.gif	gif
F	PROJECTS 2010	Project1	Idea 13 - Humorous Family Life Book	TreeHouse	Book Cover 3.jpg	jpg
F	PROJECTS 2010	Project1	Idea 13 - Humorous Family Life Book	TreeHouse	Book Cover 3.pdf	pdf
F	PROJECTS 2010	Project1	Idea 13 - Humorous Family Life Book	TreeHouse	Book Cover 3.ppt	ppt
F	PROJECTS 2010	Project1	Idea 13 - Humorous Family Life Book	TreeHouse	Book Cover 3.tif	tif
F	PROJECTS 2010	Project1	Idea 13 - Humorous Family Life Book	TreeHouse	Book Cover_Front and Back 3.ppt	ppt
F	PROJECTS 2010	Project1	Idea 13 - Humorous Family Life Book	TreeHouse	Copy of WHY DOES IT TAKE SO LONG TO BUILD A TREE HOUSE_12OCT2010.doc	doc
F	PROJECTS 2010	Project1	Idea 13 - Humorous Family Life Book	TreeHouse	Copy of WHY DOES IT TAKE SO LONG TO BUILD A TREE HOUSE_12OCT2010.pdf	pdf
F	PROJECTS 2010	Project1	Idea 13 - Humorous Family Life Book	TreeHouse	Copy of Why Does It Take So Long To Build A Tree House.doc	doc
F	PROJECTS 2010	Project1	Idea 13 - Humorous Family Life Book	TreeHouse	Dear Author.doc	doc
F	PROJECTS 2010	Project1	Idea 13 - Humorous Family Life Book	TreeHouse	Dear Parent.doc	doc
F	PROJECTS 2010	Project1	Idea 13 - Humorous Family Life Book	TreeHouse	Dear Parent2.doc	doc
F	PROJECTS 2010	Project1	Idea 13 - Humorous Family Life Book	TreeHouse	food warning.doc	doc
F	PROJECTS 2010	Project1	Idea 13 - Humorous Family Life Book	TreeHouse	FULL Book Cover.pdf	pdf
F	PROJECTS 2010	Project1	Idea 13 - Humorous Family Life Book	TreeHouse	FULL Book Cover.ppt	ppt
F	PROJECTS 2010	Project1	Idea 13 - Humorous Family Life Book	TreeHouse	Idea 13 - Humorous Family Life Book.zip	zip
F	PROJECTS 2010	Project1	Idea 13 - Humorous Family Life Book	TreeHouse	Illustration 9.doc	doc

You can use this spreadsheet for reporting out the information to your boss and sorting or analyzing it as needed.

Try this next time you have to list out files in a folder and see how much time and effort you save.

How To Compare Lists and Lookup Information In Seconds and With No Mistakes

TASK – <u>Given a parts list and a price list, figure out the cost of parts needed for producing different products and identify all the part numbers so you can order these.</u>

How to do this? You could either use –

<u>Option A</u> – Review the parts lists for each product and look for the cost and part number of each part in the price list. Write this information down or type it or copy and paste it and then calculate the total cost for the product. Repeat this multiple times for 100 products. This will take several hundred steps and several hours to complete. You may miss some or make some mistakes along the way, so you will need to double-check your work, so allow another hour or so.

Or

<u>Option B</u> – Let The Computer Do The Work.

First get both the parts lists and price list into Excel spreadsheets. **There will be more information on how to do this in the next installment, so stay tuned.**

There is a basic database function in Excel which allows you to look up values in a spreadsheet based on a key variable and the result will return corresponding data from another spreadsheet which also contains this same key variable.

So what does this mean? Sounds like complicated computer speak. But really this is something you do all the time without using a computer. This simply means that you need to know some information about your key variable (the Part which is listed in the parts list) and to do this you need to go to the price list and find the Part and then see what the price and part number is for this part. Then you take this information you found and copy it into the parts list so you can figure out the total cost and order the parts using the part numbers. You have just manually performed a database function!

Excel can do the exact same thing, but much faster and with much more accuracy. It will take a little bit of time to set this up, but once it works you can figure out the costs and part numbers for 1 product or 100 products or 10,000 products in a matter of seconds!

So how to you do this?

First, let's look at our parts list –

	A	B	C	D	E
1	**Product 1**				
2					
3	**Part**	**Quantity**	**Part Number**	**Unit Cost**	**Sub Total = Quantity X Unit Cost**
4	4 X 4 X 4 Enclosure	1			$0.00
5	6 in Rod	2			$0.00
6	8 in Wheel	4			$0.00
7	#6 Screw X 1 in.	10			$0.00
8	#6 Screw X 1 in.	12			$0.00
9					$0.00
10					

The information in the highlighted columns is what we would need to find in the price list in order to complete the table.

So, let's look at our price list –

	A	B	C
1	**Part Description**	**Part Number**	**Unit Price**
311	#10 Screw X 0.875 in.	01-000097-06	$0.16
312	#10 Screw X 5.875 in.	01-000097-07	$0.21
313	#10 Screw X 2.375 in.	01-000098-03	$0.17
314	#6 Screw X 1.25 in.	01-000098-05	$0.12
315	#10 Screw X 4.625 in.	01-000099-04	$0.20
316	#6 Screw X 5.25 in.	01-000099-07	$0.16
317	#8 Screw X 4.625 in.	01-000099-09	$0.18
318	6 in Wheel	02-001132-01	$1.10
319	8 in Wheel	02-001132-02	$1.50
320	10 in Wheel	02-001132-03	$2.50
321	6 in Rod	03-010001-13	$2.23
322	8 in Rod	03-010001-14	$3.25
323	10 in Rod	03-010001-15	$4.00
324	2 X 2 X 2 Enclosure	10-111554-02	$35.00
325	4 X 4 X 4 Enclosure	10-111554-04	$45.00
326	6 X 6 X 6 Enclosure	10-111554-06	$56.00
327	8 X 8 X 8 Enclosure	10-111554-08	$82.00

This list contains all of the parts we could possibly need. There are a total of 326 items on this list. But this is a simple example and in real life this list could have several thousand or more parts.

So let's go back to our parts list table and insert a database function into the open cells in order to have the computer lookup the missing information for us and complete the table at the click of a button.

In the first open cell, we will enter this function:

=VLOOKUP(A4, '[Parts Price

25

List.xls]Sheet1'!$A$2:$C$327,2,FALSE)

Let's figure out why we need to use this function and what it means:

VLOOKUP is an Excel database function which enables you to search for information in the Price List spreadsheet using information in the Parts List spreadsheet as your search criteria.

A4 is the cell ID of your search criteria (4 X 4 X 4 Enclosure, in this case).

'[Parts Price List.xls]Sheet1'! is the name of the spreadsheet where you are looking for the information (Parts Price List.xls, in this case).

$A$2:$C$327 is the range of data you are looking at in the Price List spreadsheet (the starting Cell ID in the top left corner, and the ending Cell ID bottom right corner of the price list data).

2 specifies the column number to look in for the data you want. The first column in the range is 1 (in this case column A is 1, column B is 2 and column C is 3. You want to specify 2 because you are looking for the Part number. If you were looking for price, you would specify 3.

A	B	C
Part Description	Part Number	Unit Price

FALSE specifies that you want to find and exact match in your search. True is the other choice and it specifies that you want to find the closest match to your search. Sometimes you might want the closest match (example you needed to find the part which is closest to ¾ inches). But for this example we need the exact match only.

So here is what this would look like entered into the cell in the Parts List where you want the results entered.

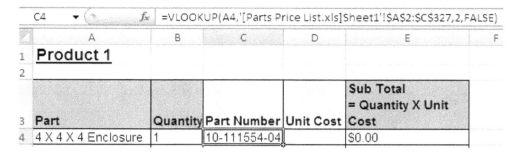

C4		fx	=VLOOKUP(A4,'[Parts Price List.xls]Sheet1'!$A$2:$C$327,2,FALSE)		
	A	B	C	D	E	F

Product 1

Part	Quantity	Part Number	Unit Cost	Sub Total = Quantity X Unit Cost
4 X 4 X 4 Enclosure	1	10-111554-04		$0.00

In the second open cell, we will enter this function to find the price (use column 3):

=VLOOKUP(A4,'[Parts Price List.xls]Sheet1'!$A$2:$C$327,3,FALSE)

D4		fx	=VLOOKUP(A4,'[Parts Price List.xls]Sheet1'!$A$2:$C$327,3,FALSE)		
	A	B	C	D	E	F

Product 1

Part	Quantity	Part Number	Unit Cost	Sub Total = Quantity X Unit Cost
4 X 4 X 4 Enclosure	1	10-111554-04	45	$45.00

Now that you have this set up, all you need to do is copy the functions down the list and you can complete the table for 1 product or 10,000 products in just a few clicks.

No looking up anything manually, no copying and pasting, and no errors!

Product 1

Part	Quantity	Part Number	Unit Cost	Sub Total = Quantity X Unit Cost
4 X 4 X 4 Enclosure	1	10-111554-04	45	$45.00
6 in Rod	2	03-010001-13	2.225	$4.45
8 in Wheel	4	02-001132-02	1.5	$6.00
#6 Screw X 1 in.	10	01-000091-02	0.1675	$1.68
#6 Screw X 1 in.	12	01-000091-02	0.1675	$2.01
				$59.14

Product 2

Part	Quantity	Part Number	Unit Cost	Sub Total = Quantity X Unit Cost
8 X 8 X 8 Enclosure	1	10-111554-08	82	$82.00
10 in Rod	2	03-010001-15	4	$8.00
8 in Wheel	4	02-001132-02	1.5	$6.00
#6 Screw X 8.125 in.	10	01-000058-00	0.19125	$1.91
#8 Screw X 3 in.	12	01-000060-06	0.16	$1.92
				$99.83

Product 3

Part	Quantity	Part Number	Unit Cost	Sub Total = Quantity X Unit Cost
4 X 4 X 4 Enclosure	1	10-111554-04	45	$45.00
6 in Rod	2	03-010001-13	2.225	$4.45
10 in Wheel	4	02-001132-03	2.5	$10.00

Try this next time you have to list out files in a folder and see how much time and effort you save.

Using WORD Forms To Create Thousands Of Documents With Just One Click.

TASK – <u>Create Product Receipts for 500+ orders which your company tracks in Excel so these can be printed and sent to the customers with their orders.</u>

How to do this? You could either use –

Option A – Create a Product Receipt document in WORD and then go to the Excel spreadsheet and find then copy and paste the information for order #1 into the WORD document then print it. Then repeat this for Order#2, Order#3…..Order#500… This will take several hundred steps and several hours to complete.   You may miss some or make some mistakes along the way, so you will need to double-check your work, so allow a few more hours or so.

Or

Option B – Let The Computer Do The Work.

First determine what information you have in the Excel spreadsheet and what information you need to include in the Product Receipt. Determine which pieces of information on Excel you will need to copy and paste into the WORD document.

Every piece of excel data contained in the cells along a row are considered part of a record. Each row of data is a record, identified by a sequential number (1, 2, 3…). Each record contains data in the cells (data fields) within the particular row. These fields are identified by the heading titles entered into the top row.

For this example, the Excel spreadsheet looks like this –

Field Names

	A	B	C	D	E	F	G	H
1	Name of Product:	Name of Customer:	Ship To Address: Street	Ship To Address: City, State, ZIP	Customer Phone:	Customer email:	Price:	Lead Time:
2	Garden planter	J. Smith	15 Spring Dr.	Middletown, OR 55214	788.222.1238	smith.j@zzz.com	$136.99	4 weeks
3	Tomato Stakes	B. Fuller	582 Mountain View Ct.	Northville, MN 44321	232.555.4321	fullerb@qqq.com	$29.95	2 weeks

Record Numbers   Data for Record #1

When the Excel spreadsheet is in the right format and you have all the field name information (Row 1) finalized, save this spreadsheet.

Then in WORD, create the Product Receipt document the way you want it to look and leave spaces for all the information you need to be included. Making the field names match the text in the WORD document, as shown below, makes it a lot easier later to map the fields correctly, but this is not required –

PRODUCT RECIPT

Name of Product:

Name of Customer:

Ship To Address:

Customer Phone:

Customer email:

Price:

Lead Time:

Ships From:

Quantity per Pack:

Weight:

Size (L X W X H):

Date Sold:

Extended Warranty Purchased:

Method of Payment:

Notes or Instructions:

Make sure you save this document.

Now comes the fun part; linking the data from the Excel Spreadsheet to the WORD document. So here we go.

Open the WORD document (Product Receipt) you created.

Then from the Mailings tab, click "Select Recipients" and Select "Use Existing List".

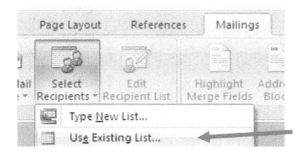

You will be prompted to select a data source. A popup window will open and you will need to navigate to the Excel file which contains the data –

Once you click on this file, you may see a screen as shown below which asks you to select the Table in the spreadsheet which contains the data you are looking for. In most cases, this will be the first sheet. The default name for this sheet is "**Sheet1$**" or if you changed the name in Excel, then you will see the names shown. Be sure to select the correct sheet or you will be looking in the wrong place for your data.

Also be sure to select the check box for "**First row of data contains column headers**". This tells WORD that the first row has the field names and not to read these as data to be placed on your WORD document.

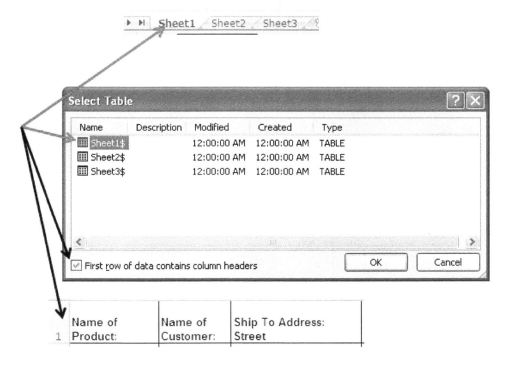

Then click "OK".

Now you can return to your WORD document and begin mapping the data fields to where you need them. To do this, first click the cursor at the point where you want to insert the data field. Then from the Mailings tab, click "**Insert Merge Field**" and then select the appropriate field from the list. The list of fields will be the names of the columns in the Excel spreadsheet.

Name of Product:	Name of Customer:	Ship To Address: Street	Ship To Address: City, State, ZIP	Customer Phone:	Customer emai :	Price:

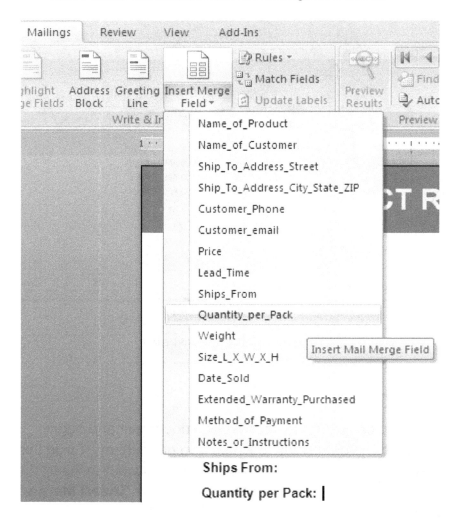

Select the field you want to insert and it will be inserted at the point in the document where you placed the cursor –

Quantity per Pack: «Quantity_per_Pack»|

Repeat this for the remaining fields you need mapped to the WORD document, then save the document.

PRODUCT RECIPT

Name of Product: «Name_of_Product»

Name of Customer: «Name_of_Customer»

Ship To Address: «Ship_To_Address_Street»

«Ship_To_Address_City_State_ZIP»

Customer Phone: «Customer_Phone»

Customer email: «Customer_email»

Price: «Price»

Lead Time: «Lead_Time»

Ships From: «Ships_From»

Quantity per Pack: «Quantity_per_Pack»

Weight: «Weight»

Size (L X W X H): «Size_L_X_W_X_H»

Date Sold: «Date_Sold»

Extended Warranty Purchased: «Extended_Warranty_Purchased»

Method of Payment: «Method_of_Payment»

Notes or Instructions: «Notes_or_Instructions»

This view displays the **<<Data_Field_Name>>** in the document, but at any time if you want to see real data, just click on "Preview Results" from the Mailings tab. This will replace the field name with live data from the record in the Excel spreadsheet.

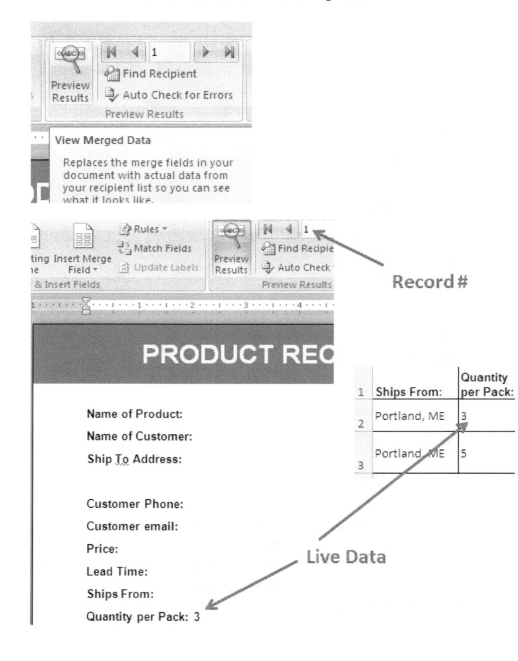

To make sure this is working, you can change the Record

number ether by:

- Clicking the arrows next to the Record number to go up or down.

- Typing in the record number you want to see in the white box.

- Searching for the record.*

*To search for a record, click "**Find Recipient**" in the Mailings tab –

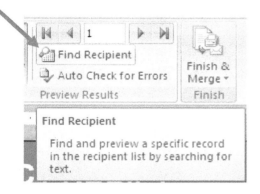

Then select the field you want to search on. In this example, we will continue with "Quantity per Pack".

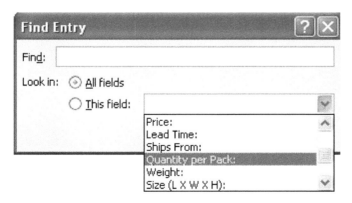

Pick this from the list and then enter the data you are looking

for in the "**Find**" field –

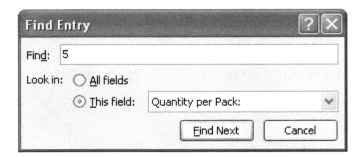

Click "Find Next" and the next record containing a Quantity per Pack of 5 will be displayed (it is Record #2 in this example) –

PRODUCT RECIPT

Name of Product: Tomato Stakes

Name of Customer: B. Fuller

Ship To Address: 582 Mountain View Ct.

　　　　　　　　　Northville, MN 44321

Customer Phone: 232.555.4321

Customer email: fullerb@qqq.com

Price: 29.95

Lead Time: 2 weeks

Ships From: Portland, ME

Quantity per Pack: 5 ⟵━━━━━━━

Weight: 2 pounds

Size (L X W X H): 36" X 2" X 2"

Date Sold: 3/8/2013

Extended Warranty Purchased: No

Method of Payment: PayPal

Notes or Instructions: Leave on Front Porch

When you are done and ready to produce these volumes of printouts for your boss, you can either make these individually by selecting specific records using the search functions shown above, or you can merge the entire set of data to however many documents as there are rows of data (i.e. 500 rows of data can be merged into a 500 page document with each page containing one record, or it can be sent to the printer to print out 500 pages - 1 for each record). Either way, this is MUCH faster than if you had to cut and paste each piece of data over from the spreadsheet.

To do this, just select "**Finish & Merge**" from the Mailings tab –

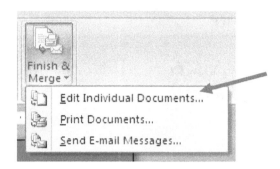

Edit individual documents will enable you to either create a new document containing all the records (1 page for each record), or you can specify the current record you are looking at in WORD, or you can pick a range of records to merge into a new document.

The new document this creates will have the data in it as part of the document and will not have the live merge fields. You will need to save this with a new name. The data fields will remain in your Product Brochure source document.

If you want all records merged into the new multipage document, select "All" or if you just want the one showing, select "Current" or Select "From" and enter in the record numbers if you want specific records printed but not all.

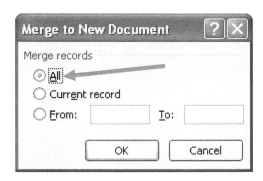

"Print Documents" will send the document to the printer rather than creating a new WORD document.

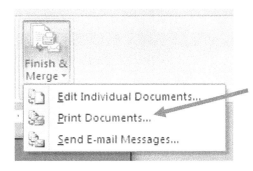

"Send E-mail Messages" will enable you to email out these documents to each Customer email address –

Try this next time you have to create multiple repetitive documents using data from an Excel spreadsheet and see how much time and effort you save. This works great for non-work documents as well. I have used it for Invitations, Thank You notes, Cards, Envelopes, Labels, Personalized crafts for school, and my favorite – making diplomas for my son's 3rd grade class (I got a copy of the class list from the teacher and pasted this into Excel to create the database to merge into the diploma – 2 minutes to create 25 diplomas – no spelling errors)!

Converting A Simple List Into a Workable Spreadsheet

TASK – <u>Take a simple plain-text list of many items and manipulate this data; sort it different ways, revise it, present it to your boss, make calculations using the information.</u>

How to do this? You could either –

<u>Option A</u> – Copy and paste each piece of information as needed into a new document and manually reformat and figure out the information needed to present. Then recheck all your work to make sure you did not miss anything or many any mistakes. If you do a good job at this, you will most likely be given a much bigger more complex list to work on next time. If you did this quickly, next time you will be expected to do it even faster. And once you submit it, there will most likely be additional requests to make changes at the very last minute.

Or

<u>Option B</u> –   Let The Computer Do The Work.

Excel can provide you with all the data functionality you need to do all of these tasks very quickly; it doesn't matter if you have 10 items or 10,000 items. But first you need to have the data in Excel.

So for this example, let's look at a very simple plain-text list. Below is a list of items needed to bring on a campout. The list beaks the items down by categories, and it also lists the weights of each item. This is very important information because when you are camping you will need to carry all of this stuff on you back to you campsite so you need keep your total packed weight to a minimum while still making sure you have packed everything you need.

==

Camping Equipment List and Weights (Plain Text List Example)

- Shorts, 4 oz.
- Extra Pair Shorts, 4 oz.
- Long Pants, 6 oz.
- 2 T-Shirts, 4 oz.
- Long Sleeve Shirt (if needed for Waterfront), 7 oz.
- Extra Shirt (optional), 4 oz.
- Sweatshirt or Fleece, 1.5 lb.
- Windbreaker, 3 lb.
- Raingear (rainsuit or poncho), 1 lb.
- Hat, 6 oz.
- Socks (3 pair minimum), 9 oz.
- Boots, 2 lb.
- Running Shoes (for around campsite), 1.5 lb.
- Shower Shoes (for showers and Waterfront), 9 oz.
- Bandannas / Handkerchiefs, 3 oz.
- Underwear, 6 oz.
- Swim Suit, 4 oz.
- Sleep Clothes, 1 lb.
- Soap in Container, 5 oz.
- Toothbrush and toothpaste, 3 oz.
- Towels (2 or more) 8 oz.
- Comb / Brush 6 oz.
- Camp mirror, 2 oz.
- Nail Clippers, 2 oz.
- Sleeping Bag, 3 lb.
- Pillow (optional), 9 oz.
- Ground Pad (optional), 10 oz.
- Extra Blanket (optional), 11 oz.

- Watch (important), 4 oz.
- Personal Medication (important), Variable
- Camera / Film, 12 oz.
- Wallet and Money, 8 oz.
- Pencil and Notepaper (important), 4 oz.
- Notebook, 8 oz.
- Pocket Knife, 6 oz.
- Flashlight / Batteries, 10 oz.
- Sunglasses, 5 oz.
- Compass, 4 oz.
- Insect Repellant (non-aerosol), 8 oz.
- Sunblock, 8 oz.
- Water Bottle, 2 lb.
- Lip Balm (optional), 2 oz.
- Repair Kit (needle, thread, etc.) (optional), 3 oz.
- Day Pack (optional), 1 lb.
- Backpack / Duffle Bag, 1 lb.
- Folding Cup (optional), 3 oz.

==

To get this text into Excel, the simplest way is to open this list in NotePad, WordPad or WORD and then simply highlight the text, then Copy it -

Next, Paste it into a blank Excel spreadsheet –

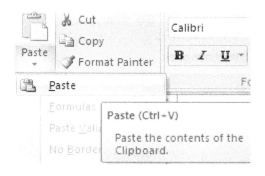

The result is that you now have this information in Excel –

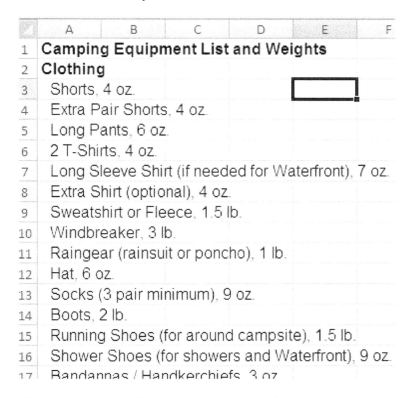

	A	B	C	D	E	F
1	**Camping Equipment List and Weights**					
2	**Clothing**					
3	Shorts, 4 oz.					
4	Extra Pair Shorts, 4 oz.					
5	Long Pants, 6 oz.					
6	2 T-Shirts, 4 oz.					
7	Long Sleeve Shirt (if needed for Waterfront), 7 oz.					
8	Extra Shirt (optional), 4 oz.					
9	Sweatshirt or Fleece, 1.5 lb.					
10	Windbreaker, 3 lb.					
11	Raingear (rainsuit or poncho), 1 lb.					
12	Hat, 6 oz.					
13	Socks (3 pair minimum), 9 oz.					
14	Boots, 2 lb.					
15	Running Shoes (for around campsite), 1.5 lb.					
16	Shower Shoes (for showers and Waterfront), 9 oz.					
17	Bandannas / Handkerchiefs, 3 oz.					

Be sure to save this spreadsheet before you move on to the next step.

Looking at the information in this list, you will notice that each line contain multiple pieces of information. Each line contains an Item Description and then a notation if it is Optional, and then at the end there is a weight for this item.

So now that you have an Excel spreadsheet containing your list, the first thing to look for is any way to break this up to make this list and make it more functional and easier to manipulate the data. From this example, it shows that every line contains text then a comma and then a weight. Since every text and weight are separated by a comma, we can use one of Excel's data functions to separate these into separate fields (or cells), which would allow us more flexibility to perform analyses and calculations on the weights, which we may need to do.

To do this, open the spreadsheet in Excel, highlight the column which contains the information, and then on the Data tab, select "**Text To Columns**"-

You will then see a window pop up which asks you if your data is Delimited or Fixed Width. This means:

Fixed width: The data can be separated by taking a fixed number of characters and putting it into a cell. You specify the number of characters using the Convert Text to Columns Wizard. This works well for data which is always the same length and in the same place. An example is if you had a list that looked like this:

COST:$20.00USD
COST:$15:00USD
COST:$05.00USD

You could specify a fixed field width filed which ended at 5 characters out for the first field "COST:"and then at 11 characters for the second field "$##.##" and then at 14 characters for the third "USD".

Field 1	Field 2	Field 3
COST	$20.00	USD
COST	$15:00	USD
COST	$05.00	USD

This is very simple to set up, but the problem is that if you have entries where the number of characters varies, then this will not work. For example –

COST:$20.00USD
COST:$150:00USD
COST:$5.00USD

Delimited Width: Specific characters appear between the fields. The most common are comma, tab or space. In this example, the weight information is separated from the description by a comma. This really helps because then it does not matter how many characters are in each piece of data, Excel will just look for the comma and break up the fields there.

So for this example, select "**Delimited**" and click "**Next >**" -

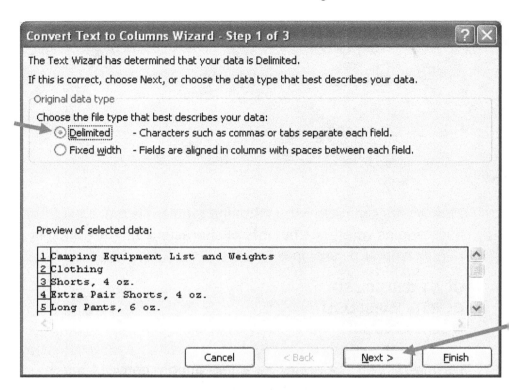

You will then see a window asking which delimiter to use. This means which character marks the separation between fields of data. In this example, we identified a comma as the delimiter. When you select the delimiter, the bottom of this window will show you how the data will be split into different fields. In this case the weight becomes separate from the description -

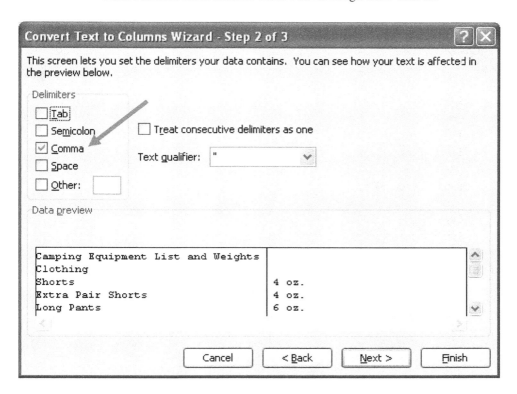

If this looks good, then click "**Next >**".

The next window will ask what type of data each column will contain -

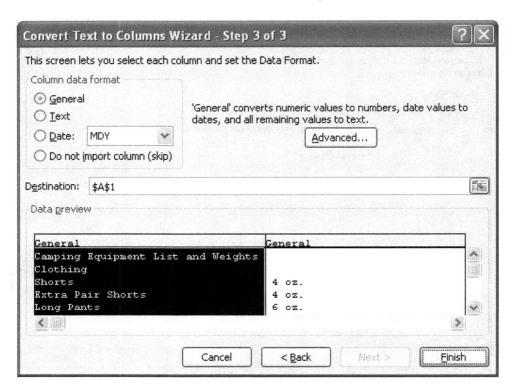

It is usually safe to leave this as "**General**" but in some cases you may want to select another type such as "**Currency**" or "**Date**" if you want it to be formatted a certain way such as $###.## or DD-MMM-YYYY. But you can always do this later if you change your mind. For now, let's just stick with "**General**" and click "**Finish >**". The result is that you now have a workable Excel spreadsheet containing the item descriptions in one column and the weights in the next –

	A	B
1	**Camping Equipment List and Weights**	
2	**Clothing**	
3	Shorts	4 oz.
4	Extra Pair Shorts	4 oz.
5	Long Pants	6 oz.
6	2 T-Shirts	4 oz.
7	Long Sleeve Shirt (if needed for Waterfront)	7 oz.
8	Extra Shirt (optional)	4 oz.
9	Sweatshirt or Fleece	1.5 lb.
10	Windbreaker	3 lb.
11	Raingear (rainsuit or poncho)	1 lb.
12	Hat	6 oz.
13	Socks (3 pair minimum)	9 oz.
14	Boots	2 lb.
15	Running Shoes (for around campsite)	1.5 lb.

Now you can use this information to provide analyses and presentations and statistics and all you need to do quickly and accurately and without any manual work!

How To Find And Present Information As Soon As Someone Asks For It

The next example builds on the previous one.

TASK – <u>Take a the list above and figure out:</u>

- How many items are optional.
- The weights of all items in ounces (oz.) so you can compare them all apples to apples. Need to convert all pounds weights into ounces.
- Sort the items by weight.
- How many Extra items there are on the list and how much these weigh.
- Total weight of all items.
- Total weight if you take out the extra items.
- Change descriptions of items separated by "/" to be clear that you need both, for example "Camera / Film" should be separate "Camera and Film".

How to do this? You could either –

<u>Option A</u> – Manually read all the information and calculate what you need, then type it into the spreadsheet or another document. Then recheck all your work to make sure you did not miss anything or many any mistakes. If you do a good job at this, you will most likely be given a much bigger more complex list to work on next time. If you did this quickly, next time you will be expected to do it even faster. And once you submit it, there will most likely be additional requests to make changes at the very last minute.

Or

<u>Option B</u> –   Let The Computer Do The Work.

With this information now in Excel you have the full capabil ties and functionality of the software to help do the tedious work for you.

Let's start with the first task – **find out how many items are optional**. If this was a list that went on for 2,500 items, it would take you a while to find all the optional items. You might lose count or lose your place in the list several times while you are doing this.

So let's automate this task. Excel has a "**FIND**" function which can locate a specific string of characters in each of the cells in this list. Do set this up in the most simple way, first create a new column called "Optional", and then in the top cell of this column, enter this function: **=FIND("optional",A3,1).** This tells Excel to find the character string "optional" inside of cell A3 starting at the first character. Copy this cell down the column to the bottom of the list.

If Excel finds the string "optional", it will display the character position where this string begins within the cell. If it does not, then it will display an error.

C3	▾	f_x =FIND("optional",A3,1)		
	A		B	C
Camping Equipment List and Weights				
Clothing				Optional
Shorts			4 oz ◈	#VALUE!
Extra Pair Shorts			4 oz.	#VALUE!
Long Pants			6 oz.	#VALUE!
2 T-Shirts			4 oz.	#VALUE!
Long Sleeve Shirt (if needed for Waterfront)			7 oz.	#VALUE!
Extra Shirt (optional)			4 oz.	14
Sweatshirt or Fleece			1.5 lb.	#VALUE!
Windbreaker			3 lb.	#VALUE!

Now let's get a little fancier and create another column called "Optional Y/N". In this column enter this function: **=IF(ISERROR(C3),"N","Y").** Copy this to all the cells in the column to the bottom of the list. This function will look at the results in the Optional column and if there is an error displayed (because the item is not optional) then this will display "N" for not optional. If there is no error (because Excel found the string "optional"), then this will display "Y"-

	D3	▼	f_x	=IF(ISERROR(C3),"N","Y")			
	A				B	C	D
1	**Camping Equipment List and Weights**						
2	**Clothing**					Optional	Optional Y/N
3	Shorts				4 oz.	#VALUE!	N
4	Extra Pair Shorts				4 oz.	#VALUE!	N
5	Long Pants				6 oz.	#VALUE!	N
6	2 T-Shirts				4 oz.	#VALUE!	N
7	Long Sleeve Shirt (if needed for Waterfront)				7 oz.	#VALUE!	N
8	Extra Shirt (optional)				4 oz.	14	Y
	Sweatshirt or Fleece				4 oz.	#VALUE!	N

Now you just need to count up all the "Y"s in this column and you will know accurately and quickly how many items are optional. Just enter this function into Excel: **=COUNTIF(D3:D54,"Y").** This tells Excel to count up all the values in the cells from D3 to D54 and display the total number which contain the text "Y". The answer is "7" in this example –

| D55 | ▼ | f_x | =COUNTIF(D3:D54,"Y") | | | |

A	B	C	D
Camping Equipment List and Weights			
Clothing		Optional	Optional Y/N
Sunblock	8 oz.	#VALUE!	N
Water Bottle	2 lb.	#VALUE!	N
Lip Balm (optional)	2 oz.	11	Y
Repair Kit (needle	thread	#VALUE!	N
Day Pack (optional)	1 lb.	11	Y
Backpack / Duffle Bag	1 lb.	#VALUE!	N
Folding Cup (optional)	3 oz.	14	Y
			7

This is a simple example, but the exact same procedure can be used for very large lists as well.

For the next question you are asked to **convert the weights to one common unit, ounces.** To do this manually you would need to:

- Determine what the units are currently
- If they are ounces, leave alone.
- If they are pounds, multiply by 16 to convert to ounces.
- Remove the unit characters so that you can make calculations using the numbers.

This can all be automated very easily.

First set up a new column for "Weight". This will display just the numeric part of the weight. Enter this function into the cells in this column: **=LEFT(B3,FIND(" ",B3,2)).** This tells Excel to display the left hand part of the entry in the cells in column B up to the point where it finds a space then stop. Since each entry if formatted to be "# unit", this will find the break easily –

C3	▼	f_x	=LEFT(B3,FIND(" ",B3,2))	

A	B	C
Camping Equipment List and Weights		
Clothing		**Weight**
Shorts	4 oz.	4
Extra Pair Shorts	4 oz.	4
Long Pants	6 oz.	6
2 T-Shirts	4 oz.	4
Long Sleeve Shirt (if needed for Waterfront)	7 oz.	7
Extra Shirt (optional)	4 oz.	4
Sweatshirt or Fleece	1.5 lb.	1.5

Now to make sure these are all ounces, make another column for "Weight (ounces)" and in this column enter this function: **=IF(RIGHT(B3,3)="oz.",C3,C3*16).** This tells Excel to look at the last 3 characters on the right hand side of the cells in column B and if they are "oz.", then take the value in column C and copy it into column D, since this is the numeric weight in ounces for the item in column A.

If the 3 right hand characters are not "oz.", in this example they will be lb. (pounds). Therefore in these cases, take the value in column C and multiply if by 16 (ounces per pound) and display the result in column D as this will be the numeric weight in ounces for the item in column A.

Now all you need to do to sort the items by weight, which is the next task, is to use the Sort function in the Data tab and sort by Column D.

First, highlight the data you want to sort, including the row containing the column headers (see below). Then Select "**Sort**" from the **Data tab**. When the sort window opens, click the checkbox for "My data has headers". This will tell Excel that the first row highlighted contains headers and should not be sorted. It also ensures that these header names will appear in the "sort By" list and make it a lot easier to figure out which one to pick -

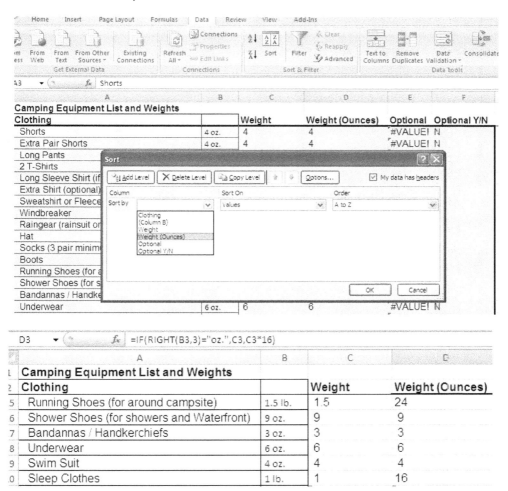

In this case, pick "Weight (Ounces)". Sort on "Values" and Order "A to Z" if you want to start with the smallest weights at the top of the list and go to the largest at the bottom -

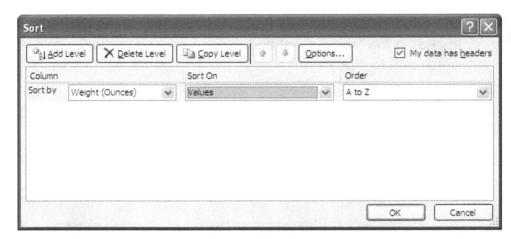

Click "Ok". If you see a "Sort Warning" window like this, select "Sort anything that looks like a number, as a number". This tells Excel to sort all the data as one list –

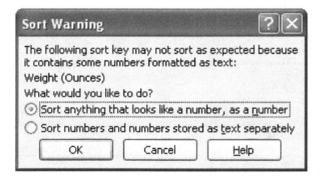

Click "Ok" and you now have sorted list –

1	Camping Equipment List and Weights			Weight	Weight (Ounces)
2				Weight	Weight (Ounces)
3	Camp mirror		2 oz.	2	2
4	Nail Clippers		2 oz.	2	2
5	Lip Balm (optional)		2 oz.	2	2
6	Bandannas / Handkerchiefs		3 oz.	3	3
7	Toothbrush and toothpaste		3 oz.	3	3
8	Folding Cup (optional)		3 oz.	3	3
9	Shorts		4 oz.	4	4
10	Extra Pair Shorts		4 oz.	4	4
11	2 T-Shirts		4 oz.	4	4
12	Extra Shirt (optional)		4 oz.	4	4
13	Swim Suit		4 oz.	4	4
14	Watch (important)		4 oz.	4	4
15	Pencil and Notepaper (important)		4 oz.	4	4
16	Compass		4 oz.	4	4
17	Soap in Container		5 oz.	5	5
18	Sunglasses		5 oz.	5	5
19	Long Pants		6 oz.	6	6
20	Hat		6 oz.	6	6
21	Underwear		6 oz.	6	6
22	Pocket Knife		6 oz.	6	6
23	Long Sleeve Shirt (if needed for Waterfront)		7 oz.	7	7
24	Wallet and Money		8 oz.	8	8
25	Notebook		8 oz.	8	8

The next question was to figure out **How Many Extra Items There Are And How Much They Weigh**.

Again if you have a very lengthy list, this can be done very easily using Excel.

First, you need to figure out which items contain the word "Extra" and then keep a running total of their weights.

So open the Excel spreadsheet, create a new column titled "Extra", and enter in a function to locate the text string "Extra" in each of the item descriptions. This function is:
=IF(ISERROR(FIND("Extra",A3,1)),"N","Y").

This time since you have more experience with this stuff, we are getting fancier and nesting the 2 functions (combining 2 functions together in one cell) we used for the last similar example of how to find optional items. In that case, we first looked for the word "optional" and then Excel generated either a location number or an error so we used a second function to translate this information into Yes/No this is optional. We set it up as 2 functions for simplicity; it's a lot easier to trouble-shoot the logic this way if it doesn't work.

But now that we are on our way to being masters of this, I have provided an example where both of these steps are combined into one function which contains both components of this logic nested together. Copy this function down to the bottom of the list. This takes the raw data and directly provides you with the "Yes/No" output you are looking for –

C3	▼	f_x =IF(ISERROR(FIND("Extra",A3,1)),"N","Y")		
	A		B	C
Camping Equipment List and Weights				
				Extra
Camp mirror			2 oz.	N
Nail Clippers			2 oz.	N
Lip Balm (optional)			2 oz.	N
Bandannas / Handkerchiefs			3 oz.	N
Toothbrush and toothpaste			3 oz.	N
Folding Cup (optional)			3 oz.	N
Shorts			4 oz.	N
Extra Pair Shorts			4 oz.	Y
2 T-Shirts			4 oz.	N
Extra Shirt (optional)			4 oz.	Y
Swim Suit			4 oz.	N
Watch (important)			4 oz	N

Now that you have identified which items are extra the second part of the question is to find out the total weight of extra items. To do this, just think how you would do it manually; you would identify which items are extra, already done, and then keep a running total of the weight of each extra item. Then just automate this process and you can figure it out for very long lists in seconds or less.

For this calculation, create a new column titled "Extra Weight" and enter in this function: **=IF(C10="N","",VALUE(F10)).**

This asks Excel to look at the Y or N values in column C (the "Extra" column you just set up) and then if the value is "N" (indicating this is not an extra item) just leave the cell blank, but if the value is not "N" (indicating this is an extra item) return the numeric value of the entry in column F (Weight (Ounces)). The result is that the Extra Weight column will contain only the weights of extra items.

D3	f_x =IF(C3="N","",F3)			
A		B	C	D
Camping Equipment List and Weights				
			Extra	Extra Weight
Camp mirror		2 oz.	N	
Nail Clippers		2 oz.	N	
Lip Balm (optional)		2 oz.	N	
Bandannas / Handkerchiefs		3 oz.	N	
Toothbrush and toothpaste		3 oz.	N	
Folding Cup (optional)		3 oz.	N	
Shorts		4 oz.	N	
Extra Pair Shorts		4 oz.	Y	4
2 T-Shirts		4 oz.	N	
Extra Shirt (optional)		4 oz.	Y	4
Swim Suit		4 oz.	N	
Watch (important)		4 oz	N	

You can then total these up using the **Sum** function to get the total weight of all extra items in ounces –

=SUM(D3:D54)			
A	B	C	D
ent List and Weights			
		Extra	Extra Weight
		N	
		N	
on (important)	Variable	N	
	thread	N	
		Total Extra wt.	41

You can also find the total weight if you remove the extra items by calculating the sum of all items (Column F) and subtracting out the Extra items (Column D). Once you set this up, you can now answer "what-if" questions if you need to know how the weight changes by making items required vs. extra. For camping, weight is very important because you need to be able to carry all this stuff for miles at a time. A common question is to figure out how to get your total to a target max weight, given the simple text list as a recommended starting point. Once you have this set up as a functional spreadsheet, this exercise takes only seconds to do. With pencil and paper, and even cutting & pasting, this is a tedious draining and aggravating process if you need to do it more than once or twice.

The next question deal with transforming data; **Change descriptions of items separated by "/" to be clear that you need both, for example "Camera / Film" should be separate "Camera and Film (you will need Both)".**

By now, you should already be thinking "how can I automate this one?" And you should recognize the logical step to follow to automate this:

1. Identify all the item descriptions which contain the character "/".

2. If the item description does contain this character:

   a. Take the first set of text before the "/"

   b. Add the word " And " to the end

   c. Follow this with the text in the description that follows "/"

   d. Add the words " (You Need Both)" to the end

3. If the description does not contain "/" then just copy it over and leave it alone.

That's it – very logical. This is what you would do manually if you did not have a computer.

Now you just need to set up a function to do this for you and it can be used to analyze lists of 10's of 1,000's of items – in just seconds.

Using a similar function as used above, first create a new column titled "Combination Items", then enter this function: **=IF(ISERROR(FIND("/",A3,2)),A3,LEFT(A3,FIND("/",A3,2)-2)&" And "&MID(A3,FIND("/",A3,2)+2,LEN(A3))& "(You Need Both)")**

Now that's a giant function!

So what exactly does it do? It does exactly what is listed above, the same thing you would do yourself if you performed this task manually.

So let's break it down to better understand how it works.

The first part is to identify which Item Descriptions contain the character "/". This is done by using the "FIND" function. This function will either return an error (if it does not find the indicated character "/") or it will return a numeric place value (if it does find the character "/") as we saw in the earlier example -

=IF(ISERROR(**FIND("/",A3,2**)),A3,LEFT(A3,FIND("/",A3,2)-2)&" And "&MID(A3,FIND("/",A3,2)+2,LEN(A3))& "(You Need Both)")

We do not want to see any errors in our results so we need an error trapping function to take care of this problem for us. If a function contains an error result and there is no error trapping, then the entire result becomes an error. This is no good. In Excel, the way to deal with this is to use the "**ISERROR**" function. This function will look at a result and if it is an error, it will return a "True" value. If the result is not an error, it will return a "False" value -

=IF(**ISERROR(FIND("/",A3,2)**),A3,LEFT(A3,FIND("/",A3,2)-2)&" And "&MID(A3,FIND("/",A3,2)+2,LEN(A3))& "(You Need Both)")

This is a very valuable function because it creates a valid result from an invalid result. The true / false result can then be used by the logical "**IF**" function to take one action of the result is true and another if it is false –

=IF(**ISERROR(FIND("/",A3,2)**),A3,LEFT(A3,FIND("/",A3,2)-2)&" And "&MID(A3,FIND("/",A3,2)+2,LEN(A3))& "(You Need Both)")

If the **ISEROR** value is True, this means the **FIND** function retuned an error, which means that Excel did not find the character "/" in the Item Description. In this case, there is no need to modify the Item Description at all and we just want to copy it over, so the action if this is true is simply copy the Item Description from the cell you are evaluating –

=IF(ISERROR(FIND("/",A3,2)),**A3**,LEFT(A3,FIND("/",A3,2)-2)&" And "&MID(A3,FIND("/",A3,2)+2,LEN(A3))& "(You Need Both)")

If the **ISERROR** value is False, this means that the **FIND** function did not return an error, which means that Excel found the character "/" in the Item Description. In this case we need to do some modification.

First we need to copy out the left hand size of the description up to but not including the "/" character. To do this we use the **LEFT** function which copies a set number of characters from the left of a sting. We want the set number to vary depending on where we find the "/", so we can use the **FIND** function for this –

=IF(ISERROR(FIND("/",A3,2)),A3,**LEFT(A3,FIND("/",A3,2)-2)**&" And "&MID(A3,FIND("/",A3,2)+2,LEN(A3))& "(You Need Both)")

Note there is a "-2" at the end of the **LEFT** function, this tells Excel to find the "/" but copy only up to 2 spaces before "/" because we do not want to copy the "/" and we do not want the space before it either, so backup 2.

Next we want to add to this first piece of text. We need to add the word " And ", with spaces before and after. We use the function "**&**" to add text stings and we need to put text and spaces into "quotes" –

=IF(ISERROR(FIND("/",A3,2)),A3,LEFT(A3,FIND("/",A3,2)-2)**&" And "**&MID(A3,FIND("/",A3,2)+2,LEN(A3))& "(You Need

Both)")

Next we need to add the part of the Item Description which follows the "/" character after the " And ", so we need to use another function to do this. You can use the **MID** function for this. **MID** copies characters from a cell beginning at a set number position and ending at a set number of positions later. In this case the beginning position is after the "/" character, so we can once again use "**FIND**" to locate this. For the ending point, we can either put in a number large enough to encompass any potential Item Description, or we can use the **LEN** function and let Excel figure out the length of the Item Description -

=IF(ISERROR(FIND("/",A3,2)),A3,LEFT(A3,FIND("/",A3,2)-2)&" And "&**MID(A3,FIND("/",A3,2)+2,LEN(A3))**)& "(You Need Both)")

For the last step, we need to take this text and add on the text "(You Need Both)", which we already know how to do by now.

And this is the final result -

Copy this function down to the bottom of the list and it will create the final text you need in seconds.

Try this next time you are given a simple list and need to do repeated multiple time consuming calculations and manipulations using the data in the list. See how much time and effort you save. This works great for any lists where you can cut and paste plain text out of, such as PDF documents, PowerPoint Presentations and Web pages.   I have used it for Parts lists, inventory sheets, financial statements, as well as basketball rosters and party planning lists. I was able to copy and paste a list of my son's basketball team roster and schedule off the web and quickly figure out player lineups and what-if scenarios based on rankings and total floor time. If a player did not show up at game time, I could quickly recalculate the stat sheets in seconds

– no spelling errors, no math mistakes! The other coaches were still struggling with pads and pens and clipboards and madly crossing out stuff while the game officials impatiently looked on. Why put yourself through this when there are tools to help you out?

BONUS #1: Excel Pivot Tables That Automate Tasks You No Longer Have Time For

One of the most valuable data management tools commonly available to many people is MS Excel. In addition to its ability to produce detailed charts and perform calculations, it also has the capability to produce pivot tables which are user defined summary tables which can be used to present voluminous information in different ways which enable decisions to be made quickly and effectively. Pivot tables provide valuable data analyses real time in a visual format. This is ideal for presentations to higher level management people who are big-picture focused and do not have time nor interest in evaluating numbers and pieces of data.

Pivot tables basically enable you to corral your data into a format that is instantly meaningful, and it allows you to be able to change around the format instantly as needed to provide the valuable informant needed by your organization. This is one of those magic tools that enables you to complete major tedious tasks in seconds rather than spending hours, or days on them. Pivot tables provide the much needed interface between the low level details (the raw data) and the high level decision making tools (an organized presentation of information that all the higher-ups can relate to).

If you can present information in pivot tables you will be able to provide a valuable service to you organization and you will be getting the most work done in the least time. Put the computers to work, let them do the time consuming mindless stuff for you. You will see your productivity, your value and your outlook on life improve.

What follows are real life detailed examples of data management assignments tasks which have been presented using Excel pivot tables.

Give it a try – you have nothing to lose!

How To Instantly Manage User Accounts

TASK – <u>Identify all of the 3,000+ system users you have Reviewer Access.</u>

<u>Situation</u>: "Review" type account licenses cost a lot of $$$, so your company needs to limit who has these accounts to those who truly need it. In addition, the compliance auditor is concerned about too many people having access to sensitive data so this is another reason to see who has this access and limit it. This used to be the shared responsibilities of 3 middle managers who managed the different areas, but they are all gone now and you are next in line to have this responsibility for the entire system, plus what you were doing before the managers suddenly left.

How to do this? You could either use –

Option A – Export the report from the system and highlight each account type in a different color, or sort it by account type. This will result in a long list which high level people will tune out, so you will need to summarize the results you find and set up a table or chart to show management what you found. After you do this, they will probably have questions which require you to do more work (such as "when was the last time each of these people logged into the system?"). This will force you to go back and start the chart over again, and again, and again... until you have figured out what they want. You may miss some information or make some mistakes along the way, so you will need to double-check your work, so allow more time for proofreading.

Or

Option B – **Let The Computer Do The Work**.

Export the data into Excel and set up a pivot table to present the information in an organized manner which highlights what management is looking for; who has the high level accounts and when did they last use the system?

The system outputs a report with these fields:

- User ID
- Name: Last, First
- Email address
- Last login time (includes date and time)
- Account access group (system access level)
- Account group description (explanation of the group)
- User status (active of inactive – locked out due to incorrect password entered too many times).

This is all really valuable information, but there are over 20,000 rows in this table. You could spend a day just figuring out who is a reviewer and who is not. Then you could spend another day figuring how many reviewers belong to what group. And then you need to figure out which reviewers have been using the system and which have not touched it for a while.

User ID	Last Name	First Name	Email Address	Account Type	Account Access Group	Account Group Description	Last Login Time	User State
00771383	Brown	Jane	j.brown@qxmbck.com	review	review_doc	Contributor	6/10/2013 20:29	Active
00771804	Smith	Michael	m.smith@qxmbck.com	review	review_doc	Reviewer	6/14/2013 3:49	Active
00771158	Kopp	Erik	e.kopp@qxmbck.com	review	review_doc	Contributor	5/31/2013 13:41	Active
00779605	North	Daniel	d.north@qxmbck.com	review	review_doc	Contributor	6/17/2013 9:45	Active
00013775	Connors	Stanley	s.connors@qxmbck.com	review	review_doc_leg	Legal Review	6/12/2013 0:26	Active
00026498	Jones	Mary	m.jones@qxmbck.com	review	review_doc_qc	Quality Release	4/29/2013 9:49	Active
00026498	Jones	Mary	m.jones@qxmbck.com	view	view_doc_qc	Quality Inspector	4/29/2013 9:49	Active
00045309	Wilson	Sally	s.wilson@qxmbck.com	review	review_doc	Contributor	6/13/2013 20:50	Active
00058261	West	John	j.west@qxmbck.com	review	review_doc	Reviewer	6/14/2013 10:07	Active
00068456	Chen	Christopher	c.chen@qxmbck.com	review	review_doc	Contributor	7/24/2012 12:18	Active
00771383	Brown	Jane	j.brown@qxmbck.com	review	review_doc_qc	Quality Release	2/18/2013 2:38	Active
00771804	Smith	Michael	m.smith@qxmbck.com	review	review_doc	Reviewer	1/5/2012 14:21	Active
00771158	Kopp	Erik	e.kopp@qxmbck.com	review	review_doc_prod	Production Shift Super	12/12/2012 9:33	Active
00779605	North	Daniel	d.north@qxmbck.com	review	review_doc	Contributor	6/6/2013 12:36	Active

So let's try another approach and let Excel organize the data for you using a pivot table.

To do this, first click on the "Insert" tab at the top of the page:

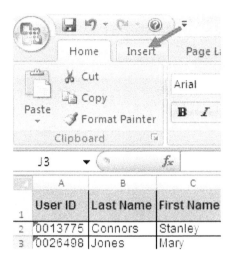

Next, click on any cell within the table of data (you can click on any cell within the table, but it must be within the table – you'll see why in a second):

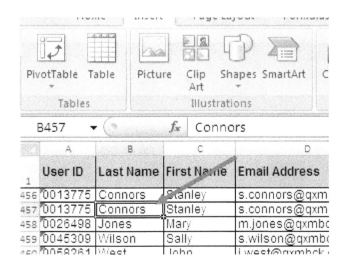

Then, click the "Pivot Table" button:

When you click the "Pivot Table" button, the Create Pivot Table window will open as shown. If you have clicked first on a cell within the table, as we mentioned above, the Table/Range will already be populated with the data source (range of cells encompassing the table):

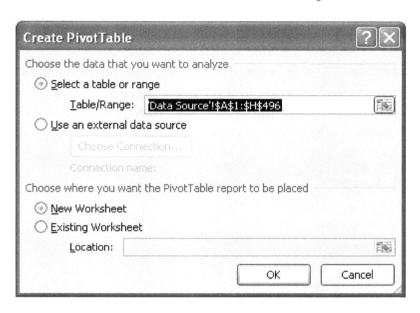

If you did not click within the table first, this will be blank and you will need to enter this manually. Note: You can always type in the range if you want to change it:

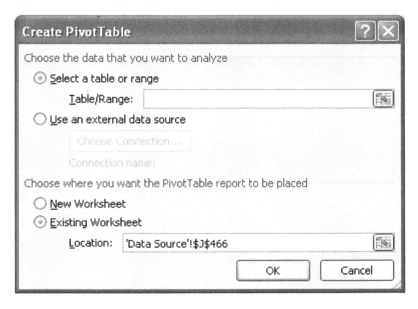

So let's go back to the first window and accept the entire table data range. Also, set the pivot table to be placed into a New Worksheet. This keeps things simpler and sets up the pivot table on another tab and leaves the source data alone. This also allows you to easily delete the other worksheet tabs if you need to get rid of the pivot table and start over without messing up the source data. Then click "OK":

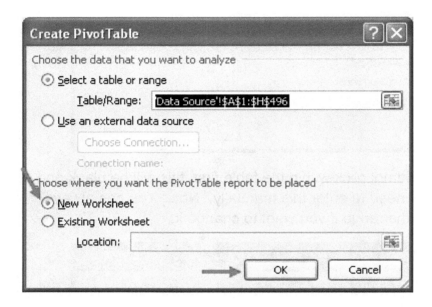

You will then see a screen which looks something like this:

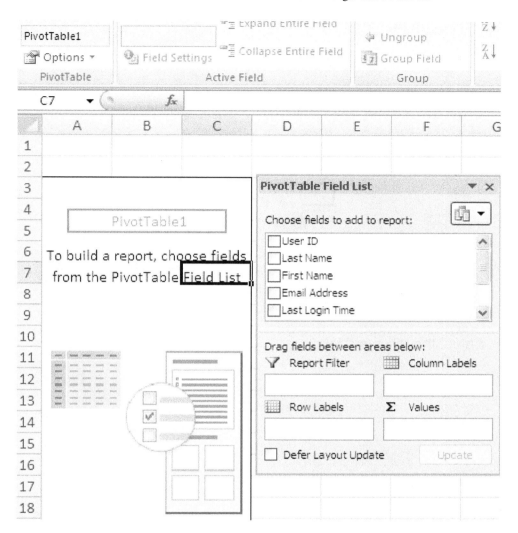

Right-click on the area that says "PivotTable1" and select "Pivot Table Options":

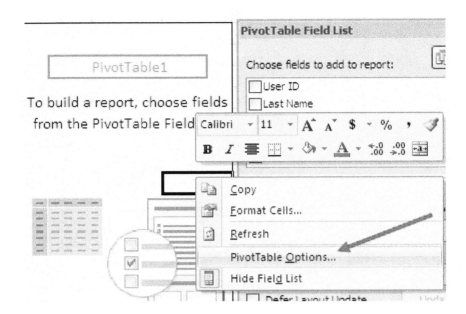

Select the "Display" tab:

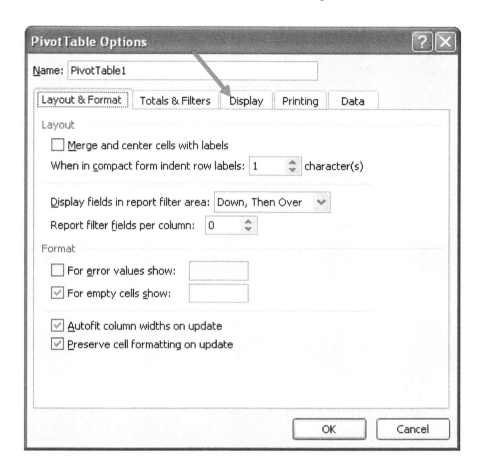

Then make sure the box is checked for "Classic Pivot Table Layout". This is one of the most valuable functions of the pivot table to be able to drag data fields around within the table. This allows you to reformat it on the fly and provide answers to what-if questions in seconds. Click "OK" when this is done:

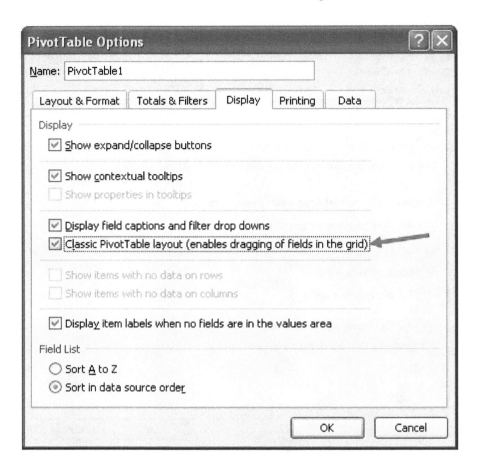

Then you will have a screen that looks like this:

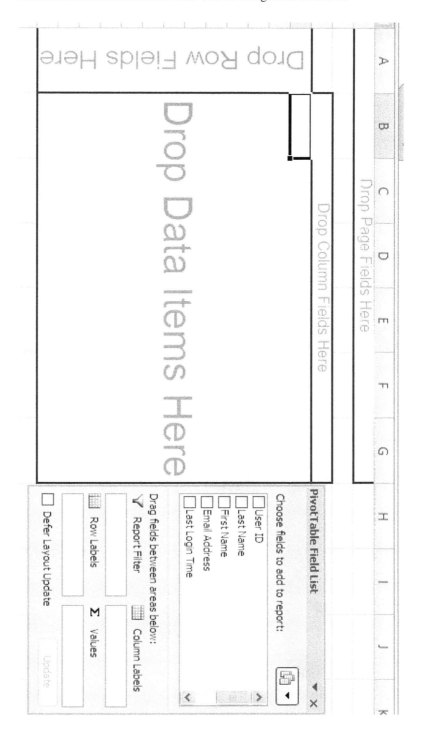

Please note that if you click on a cell outside of the pivot table, the field list window and the text disappear:

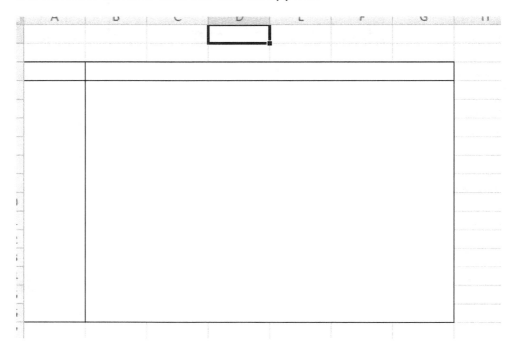

If this happens, just go back and click on one of the cells inside the pivot table and it will all reappear. If it does not reappear, right-click on a cell in the pivot table and make sure "Show Field List" is selected:

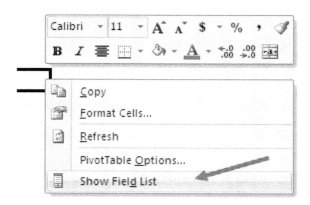

Now you are ready to set up your pivot table. Remember, whatever you set up can be very easily and quickly modified on the fly as needed. So this is just the initial set up and not going to cost you any time later if you want to change it around. That's one of the beauties of the pivot table. It's like arranging cards on a table, you can slide them around in any order you want very quickly.

The first thing you need to do is to look at the field list and check all the boxes next to information you want to be displayed in the pivot table. In this example, we want to include user ID, name, account type, and last login. You can always uncheck these if you do not want them or check them if you want them again, or go back and add more fields later.

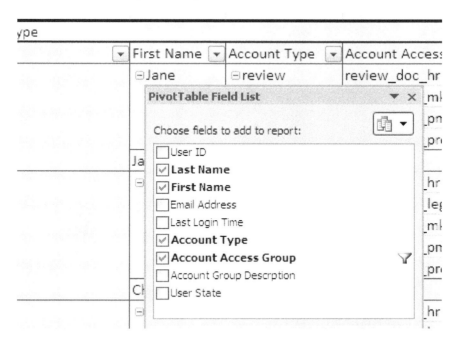

For now, let's stick with these and see what our pivot table looks like. You will see that the columns in the table show each of the data fields we selected, in the order we selected them:

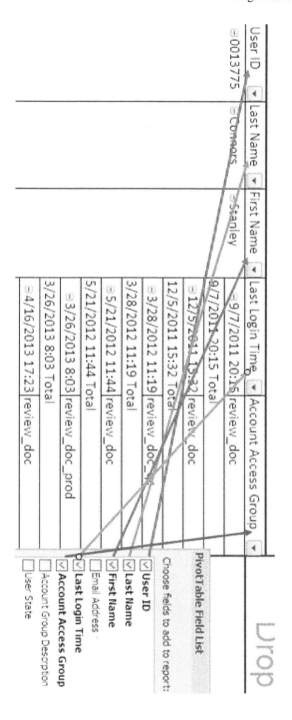

If you want to change the order of the columns around, there are 3 ways to do this:

1. In the Pivot Table click on the Column Title (field name) and drag it to where you want it.
2. In the Pivot Table Field List window, click on the Row Label you want to move and drag it to where you want to move it.
3. In the Pivot Table List, uncheck the fields and re-check them in the order you want.

I told you pivot tables are very flexible.

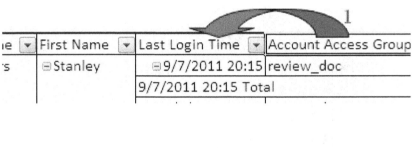

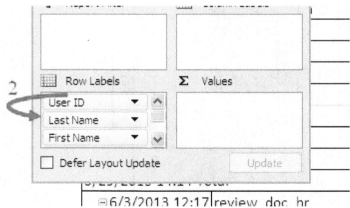

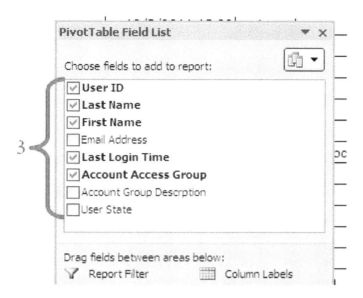

To not drive you crazy with this example, I am going to move forward with the focus on setting up the pivot table to accomplish the 2 objectives set forth by management:

1. Identify how many people have Reviewer accounts.

2. Identify who the people are with Reviewer accounts and when they last used the system.

Beyond this, you are welcome to customize the look and feel of the pivot table and experiment with all the features and cool stuff it can do, but for now let's move on with the primary objectives. Everyone will develop their own style with these once you become familiar with the basic workings of pivot tables.

One thing we have not yet explained in the large are to the right which says "Drop Data Items Here":

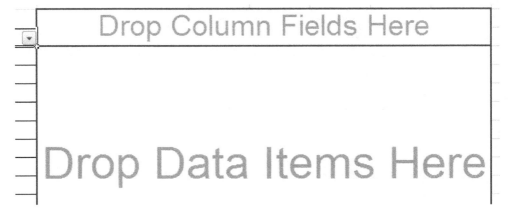

This area lets you tally up items in each field and is handy for showing how many lower level items relate to a higher level item. For this example, we can drag "Account Access Group" into this area and the pivot table will tell us how many accounts (low level data) are related to each user (high level data) since each user may have multiple accounts in the system for dong different things. Management may want to see this for example if they are considering limiting Reviewer access and see that some reviewers also have other accounts. So let's do this:

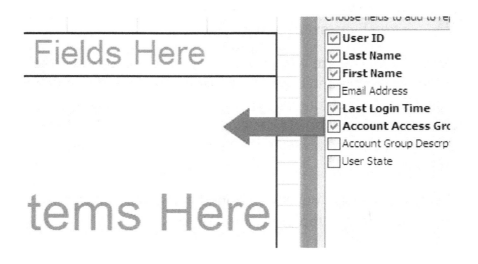

By dragging over "Account Access Group" the pivot table now displays a count of account access groups related to each user ID. You will quickly see which users have multiple accounts in the system and what they are:

Count of Use

User ID	Last Name	First Name	Account Access Group	Account Group Descrption	Total
0026498	Jones	Mary	admin_sys	admin	1
				DBA Account	1
			admin_sys Total		2
			approve_doc		1
			review_doc	Contributor	2
				Reviewer	1
			review_doc Total		3

Let's get back to the first objective and figure out how many users have review accounts. To do this, let's place **Account Type** in the leftmost column, followed user name, **Account Access Group**, and then a count of **Account Type**. This is what the table will look like:

Count of Account Type				
Account Type ▾	Last Name ▾	First Name ▾	Account Access Group ▾	Total
⊟ review	⊟ Brown	⊟ Jane	review_doc_hr	1
			review_doc_mkt	1
			review_doc_pm	2
			review_doc_prod	3
		Jane Total		7
	⊟ Chen	⊟ Christopher	review_doc_hr	1
			review_doc_leg	2
			review_doc_mkt	1
			review_doc_pm	1
			review_doc_prod	5
		Christopher Total		10

This is what the table definition looks like:

At the bottom of the table, the Total number of review accounts is displayed.

	Sally Total	5
review Total		62

If you want to display the totals for the individuals (how many review accounts does each person have) or total review accounts for all, right click in the field and select field settings:

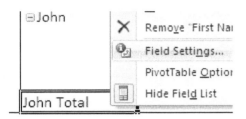

On the Subtotals & Filters tab, select "Automatic". The example below will enable the total count of Review Accounts for each First name:

The result is shown in the table:

⊟ Smith	⊟ Michael	review_doc_hr	1
		review_doc_mkt	1
		review_doc_pm	1
		review_doc_prod	3
	Michael Total		6
⊟ West	⊟ John	review_doc_hr	1
		review_doc_leg	2
		review_doc_pm	1
		review_doc_prod	3
	John Total		7
⊟ Wilson	⊟ Sally	review_doc_hr	1
		review_doc_leg	1
		review_doc_prod	3
	Sally Total		5

This applies to all users.

If you want the total of all Review accounts to be displayed, click on the Account type field and select "Field Settings":

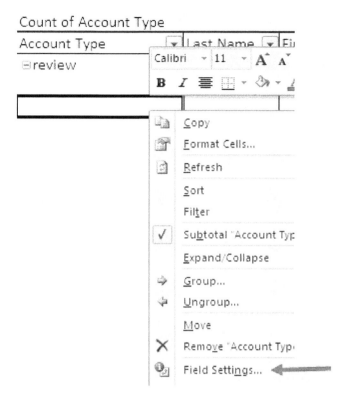

Then set the Subtotal & Filter to "Automatic":

If you present this information and are then asked more detailed questions, let's say "How many marketing review accounts are active?", then you can filter the table to only show marketing review accounts. To do this, we can click the filter arrow next to the Account access Group, then select "review_doc_mkt" from the list and unselect all others:

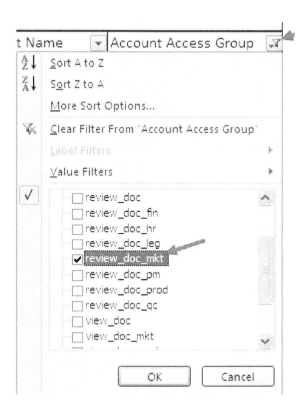

Then "OK":

You now have a simple summary table showing how many marketing review accounts are assigned to which users:

Count of Account Type				
Account Type ▼	Last Name ▼	First Name ▼	Account Access Group 🔽	Total
⊟review	⊟Brown	⊟Jane	review_doc_mkt	1
		Jane Total		1
	⊟Chen	⊟Christopher	review_doc_mkt	1
		Christopher Total		1
	⊟Connors	⊟Stanley	review_doc_mkt	2
		Stanley Total		2
	⊟Smith	⊟Michael	review_doc_mkt	1
		Michael Total		1
review Total				5

To make this look even simpler, you may not need to know how many accounts each user has (the line that says "Total" after each name) so you can disable this by right clicking in one of these cells and selecting Field Settings:

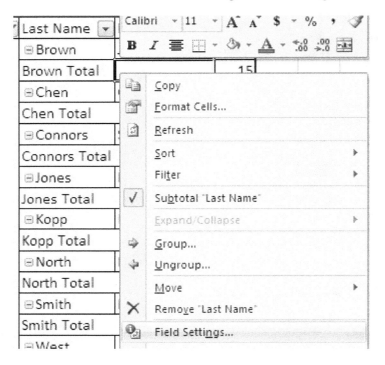

Then checking the box by "None" under subtotals:

The result looks a lot cleaner:

Count of Account Type				
Account Type	Last Name	First Name	Account Access Group	Total
⊟review	⊟Brown	⊟Jane	review_doc_mkt	1
	⊟Chen	⊟Christopher	review_doc_mkt	1
	⊟Connors	⊟Stanley	review_doc_mkt	2
	⊟Smith	⊟Michael	review_doc_mkt	1
review Total				5

Now for the second objective (when did these people last log on?), we need to add in one more field to the table. To do this, use one of the 3 options noted above to add in the field "Last Login Time" and you will see the last login time for all users who have Marketing Review accounts:

unt of Account Type

count Type		Last Name	First Name	Last Login Time	Account Access Group	
review		⊟ Brown	⊟ Jane	⊟ 5/1/2013 13:33	review_doc_mkt	
		⊟ Chen	⊟ Christopher	⊟ 6/13/2013 20:40	review_doc_mkt	
		⊟ Smith	⊟ Michael	⊟ 5/29/2013 19:03	review_doc_mkt	
view Total						

PivotTable Field List

Choose fields to add to report:

- ☐ User ID
- ☑ **Last Name**
- ☑ **First Name**
- ☐ Email Address
- ☑ **Last Login Time**
- ☑ **Account Type**
- ☑ **Account Access Group**
- ☐ Account Group Descrption
- ☐ User State

Now, let's say management asked for one more piece of information to be added – location. They want to know the sites where these users are located. Let's say you can obtain a list of locations:

User ID	Name	Location
0013775	Stanley Connors	Headquarters
0026498	Mary Jones	NYC Office
0045309	Sally Wilson	Phoenix
0058261	John West	Denver
0068456	Christopher Chen	Chicago
0071383	Jane Brown	Boston
0071804	Michael Smith	Atlanta
0077158	Erik Kopp	Headquarters
0079605	Daniel North	Toronto

As we discussed in Volume 1, we do not need to type in any of this information into the data. Using the VLOOKUP function, you can automate the addition of location into your spreadsheet, but you need to find a "key" (something that appears in both lists which you can use to match the person in both lists). In this cast, User ID is the key since it appears in both lists in exactly the same format so Excel can identify this easily when looking from one list to the other:

User ID	Last Name	First Name	Email Address
0013775	Connors	Stanley	s.connors@qxml
0026498	Jones	Mary	m.jones@qxmbc
0026498	Jones	Mary	m.jones@qxmbc
0026498	Jones	Mary	m.jones@qxmbc
0045309	Wilson	Sally	s.wilson@qxmbc
0059261	West	John	j.west@qxmbck

So, let's add in location. First set up a new column for this information:

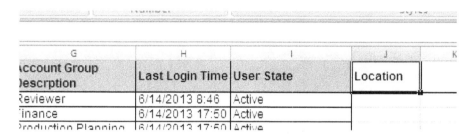

G	H	I	J	K
Account Group Descrption	Last Login Time	User State	Location	
Reviewer	6/14/2013 8:46	Active		
Finance	6/14/2013 17:50	Active		
Production Planning	6/14/2013 17:50	Active		

Then in the first cell of this column, type in this function:

=VLOOKUP(A2,Location!$A$2:$C$10,3,FALSE)

VLOOKUP tells Excel to look for information from a list in a specified location.

"A2" is the cell which contains the User ID – the key.

"Location!" is the name of the worksheet tab in the spreadsheet which contains the location information needed:

$A2:$C$10 is the range where the location data can be found.

This must include the User ID and the location:

	A	B	C
1	User ID	Name	Location
2	0013775	Stanley Connors	Headquarters
3	0026498	Mary Jones	NYC Office
4	0045309	Sally Wilson	Phoenix
5	0058261	John West	Denver
6	0068456	Christopher Chen	Chicago
7	0071383	Jane Brown	Boston
8	0071804	Michael Smith	Atlanta
9	0077158	Erik Kopp	Headquarters
10	0079605	Daniel North	Toronto

3 is the index, how many spaces Excel needs to count over (the key column counts as 1):

This will return the corresponding location for the User ID in column A:

`=VLOOKUP(A2,Location!$A$2:$C$10,3,FALSE)`

s	Account Type	Account Access Group	Account Group Descrption	Last Login Time	User State	Location
xmbck.com	review	review_doc	Reviewer	6/14/2013 8:46	Active	Headquarters
nbck.com	review	review_doc_fin	Finance	6/14/2013 17:50	Active	

Make sure the range includes "$" before each column and row ID ($A2:$C$10). This keeps the range from changing when you copy this function to other cells. You do not want this range to change because the lookup data is in a fixed location.

Now you just need to copy the first cell in the Location column down to the bottom of the list:

ss	Account Group Descrption	Last Login Time	User State	Location
	Reviewer	6/14/2013 8:46	Active	Headquarters
า	Finance	6/14/2013 17:50	Active	NYC Office
d	Production Planning	6/14/2013 17:50	Active	NYC Office
r	Human Resources	6/14/2013 17:50	Active	NYC Office
า	Finance	7/6/2012 12:37	Inactive and Locked	Phoenix
c	Quality Release	6/14/2013 18:39	Active	Denver
า	Trainer	6/14/2013 18:39	Active	Denver
	External User	6/14/2013 18:39	Active	Denver
	DBA Account	6/14/2013 18:39	Active	Denver
	Quality Inspector	6/14/2013 18:39	Active	Denver
า	Trainer	6/14/2013 18:25	Active	Chicago
:	Field Sales	6/14/2013 18:25	Active	Chicago
า	Finance	6/17/2013 12:27	Active	Boston
	External User	6/17/2013 12:27	Active	Boston
	DBA Account	6/17/2013 12:27	Active	Boston
m	Project Management	6/17/2013 12:27	Active	Boston
า	Finance	7/12/2012 8:51	Inactive and Locked	Atlanta
	Contributor	6/17/2013 6:28	Active	Headquarters
	External User	6/17/2013 11:45	Active	Toronto
า	Trainer	6/11/2013 11:57	Active	Headquarters
	Read Only	2/24/2011 14:28	Active	NYC Office
rod	Warehouse	2/25/2013 20:37	Active	Phoenix
	Read Only	6/15/2011 14:38	Active	Denver
า	Trainer	6/14/2013 13:29	Active	Chicago
rod	Warehouse	6/14/2013 13:29	Active	Chicago
	admin	11/28/2012 3:30	Active	Boston

Once you have this if you are happy with the results, I strongly recommend copying these cells and pasting as values. This removes the function from the spreadsheet. Currently these cells displaying the locations all contain live links. If you click on any of the location cells, you will see that the contents are a function:

=VLOOKUP(A5,Location!$A$2:$C$10,3,FALSE)			
D	I	J	K
ess	User State	Location	
ꓱqxmbck.com	Active	Headquarters	
ıxmbck.com	Active	NYC Office	
ıxmbck.com	Active	NYC Office	
ıxmbck.com	Active	NYC Office	
ꓱxmbck.com	Inactive and Locked	Phoenix	
nbck com	Active	Denver	

These can change if the source data is altered or may become errors if you decide to delete the source data:

H	I	J
st Login Time	User State	Location
14/2013 8:46	Active	#N/A
14/2013 17:50	Active	#N/A
14/2013 17:50	Active	#N/A
14/2013 17:50	Active	#N/A
ꓱ/2012 12:37	Inactive and Locked	#N/A
14/2013 18:39	Active	#N/A
14/2013 18:39	Active	#N/A
14/2013 18:39	Active	#N/A

The functions also take up more memory and make the file size bigger and they make opening the file slower because Excel has to lookup all the data over again each time you open the spreadsheet, So there are many reasons to remove the functions and keep the resulting data. To do this, simply highlight all the cells in the column and select Copy, then select "Paste Values":

This causes the contents of the cells to be the resulting values rather than the function:

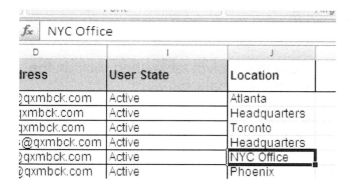

lress	User State	Location
)qxmbck.com	Active	Atlanta
)xmbck.com	Active	Headquarters
)xmbck.com	Active	Toronto
:@qxmbck.com	Active	Headquarters
)qxmbck.com	Active	NYC Office
)qxmbck.com	Active	Phoenix

Once you have this information added to the source data, you need to add it to the pivot table. You will notice that Location does not appear on the list of fields, but it is now part of the source data:

⊟Jane	⊟5/1/2013 13:33	review_doc_
⊟Christopher	⊟6/13/2013 20:40	review_doc_
⊟Michael	⊟5/29/2013 19:03	review_doc_

PivotTable Field List

Choose fields to add to report:

- ☐ User ID
- ☑ **Last Name**
- ☑ **First Name**
- ☐ Email Address
- ☑ **Last Login Time**
- ☑ **Account Type**
- ☑ **Account Access Group**
- ☐ Account Group Descrption
- ☐ User State

To fix this, click on any cell in the pivot table, then click on the Options tab, and select "Change Data Source":

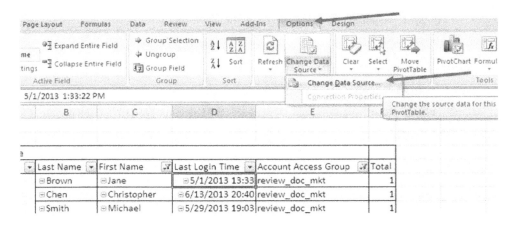

When the data source and range are displayed, make sure the range covers all of the data you want to include. In this example, we want to be sure the range includes the new column "J":

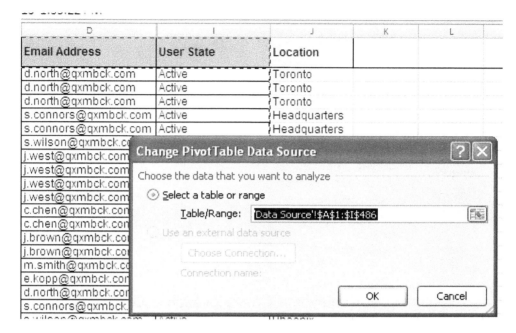

You can either highlight all the cells again, o just type in "J" in place of "I" Then click "OK":

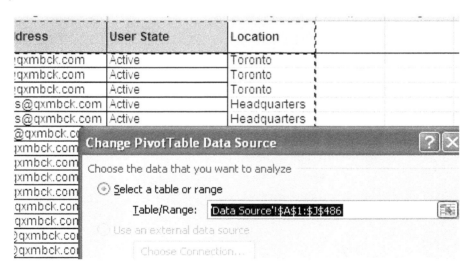

Now you can go back to the pivot table and you will see

location is added:

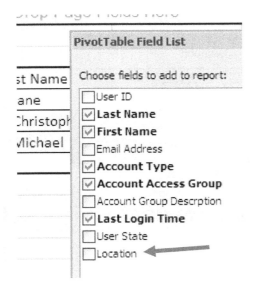

So, check this box and you will have location added to the pivot table:

t of Account Type					
unt Type	Last Name	First Name	Location	Last Login Time	Account Access Gr
'iew	⊟Brown	⊟Jane	⊟Boston	⊟5/1/2013 13:33	review_doc_mkt
	⊟Chen	⊟Christopher	⊟Chicago	⊟6/13/2013 20:40	review_doc_mkt
	⊟Smith	⊟Michael	⊟Atlanta	⊟5/29/2013 19:03	review_doc_mkt

Now let's say, you are told the Chicago office recently moved to St. Louis and the table needs to be updated. So, you just go back to the source data, highlight the location cells, and replace "Chicago" with "St. Louis":

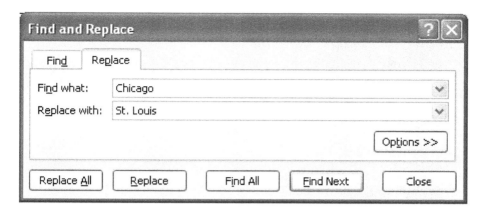

The data source is not up to date:

But, the pivot table still shows Chicago:

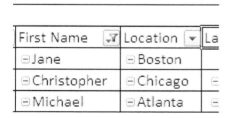

To fix this, right click on any cell in the pivot table and click on "Refresh":

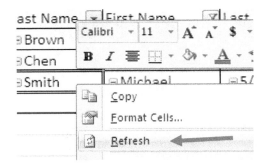

This causes Excel to update the pivot table and lookup the source data again. Now you will see the new information:

The last thing you might want to also do to make this presentation shine even more is to create a pivot chart. To do this, go back to your source data, and under the Insert tab, chose Pivot Chart:

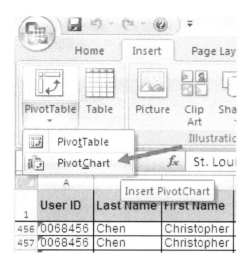

Follow the same set up as with the pivot table:

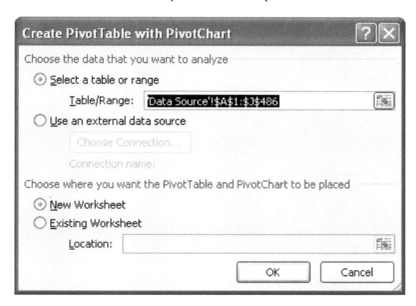

For this chart, let's make a simple graph showing the number of accounts by type. Select the **Account Type** field:

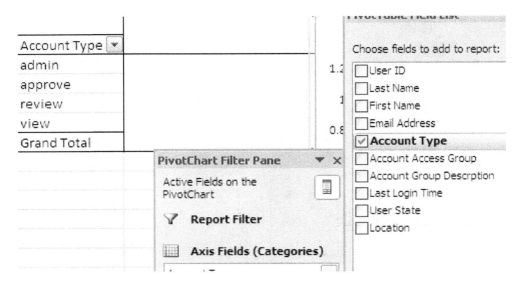

Then drag this field into the Σ Values box so the chart will show the count for each account type:

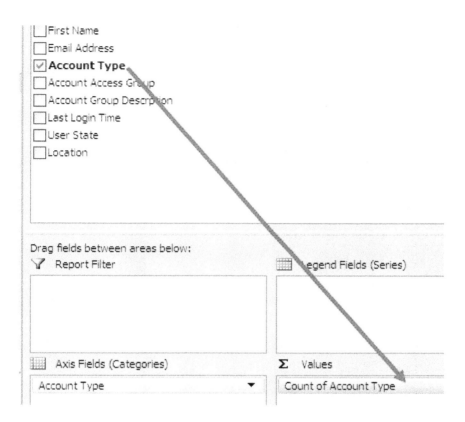

You now have a nice presentation to show management how many of ach account type are in the system, and it only took you 5 seconds to set this up!

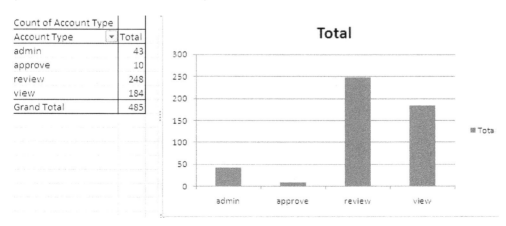

If you need to make any changes to this chart, you can right click on the chart and edit as you would any Excel chart:

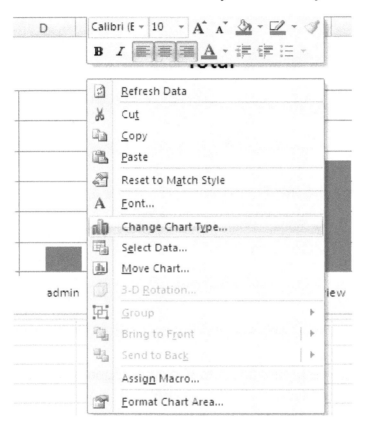

Total time spent to do this – 3 seconds!!

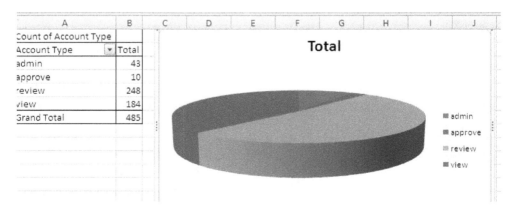

You can then take this chart and cut and paste it into a PowerPoint presentation, email, or Word document – all in under 5 seconds!!!

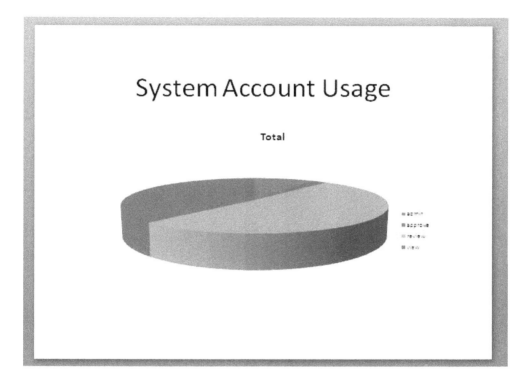

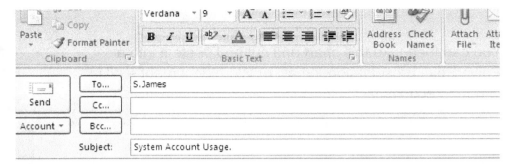

A detailed analysis of the system usage shows the majority of users have Review access -

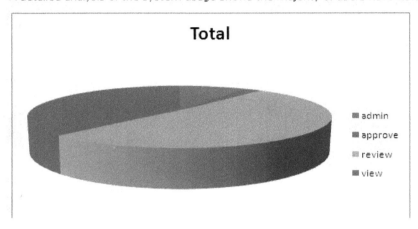

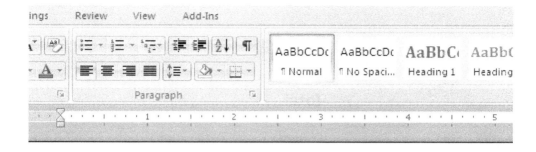

This is the current system account usage breakdown -

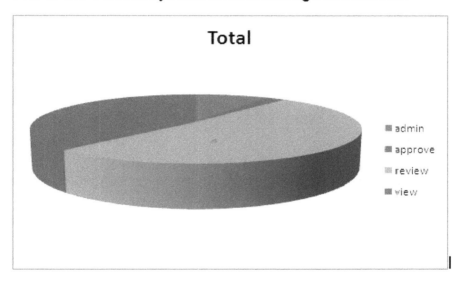

And even after you cut and paste it into another document, you can still modify it as needed:

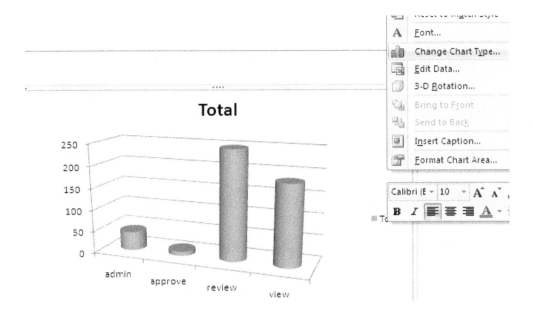

Now this is productivity at its max!

How To Instantly Manage Parts Lists

TASK – <u>Provide An Urgently Needed Quick Summary of all of the 3,000+ Product Assemblies Produced Using Certain Components.</u>

<u>Situation</u>: You have a list of 10,000+ products made by your company including the components, quantities and costs used in each. You need to provide a very quick but accurate summary of which products use certain components as your company is currently in contract negotiations with different suppliers of some of these components and needs to make a decision this morning to award the bid to a new supplier. This could save over $1Million in costs but the deal must close at noon today. Originally these components were not on the table for negotiation, but in a last minute attempt to win business, a new supplier has promised favorable [pricing if the deal signed today.

How to do this? You could either use –

Option A – Review the list and highlight each component type in a different color, or sort it by component type. Then you can total up the components and enter these numbers into a chart to make a presentation for management. After you do this, they will probably have questions which require you to do more work (such as "how many of each component goes into each product?", or "what if we only focus on components B and C but not A?"). This will force you to go back and start the chart over again, and again, and again…until you have figured out what they want. You may miss some information or make some mistakes along the way, so you will need to double-check your work, so allow more time for proofreading.

Or

Option B – Let The Computer Do The Work.

First look at the list and see what information you have:

Product	Part	Quantity	Part Number	Unit Cost	Cost
Product 1	4 X 4 X 4 Enclosure	1	10-111554-04	$45.00	$45.00
Product 1	6 in Rod	2	03-010001-13	$2.23	$4.45
Product 1	8 in Wheel	4	02-001132-02	$1.50	$6.00
Product 1	#6 Screw X 1 in.	10	01-000091-02	$0.17	$1.68
Product 1	#6 Screw X 1 in.	12	01-000091-02	$0.17	$2.01
Product 1	TOTAL				$59.14
Product 2	8 X 8 X 8 Enclosure	1	10-111554-08	$82.00	$82.00
Product 2	10 in Rod	2	03-010001-15	$4.00	$8.00
Product 2	8 in Wheel	4	02-001132-02	$1.50	$6.00
Product 2	#6 Screw X 8.125 in.	10	01-000058-00	$0.19	$1.91
Product 2	#8 Screw X 3 in.	12	01-000060-06	$0.16	$1.92
Product 2	TOTAL				$99.83
Product 3	4 X 4 X 4 Enclosure	1	10-111554-04	$45.00	$45.00
Product 3	6 in Rod	2	03-010001-13	$2.23	$4.45
Product 3	10 in Wheel	4	02-001132-03	$2.50	$10.00
Product 3	#10 Screw X 10 in.	10	01-000069-04	$0.25	$2.50
Product 3	#10 Screw X 3.75 in.	12	01-000076-02	$0.19	$2.25
Product 3	TOTAL				$64.20

This is a very simple example for illustration purposes, but the same logical steps apply to large and more complex lists.

Using pivot tables as described above, you can easily set up a pivot table with this data to show each component in the left hand column, followed by which products it is used with and the quantities and costs of the components used in each product:

Part Number	Part	Product	Quantity	Unit Co	Cost
⊟01-000058-00	⊟#6 Screw X 8.125 in.	⊟Product 2	⊟10	⊟$0.19	$1.91
⊟01-000060-06	⊟#8 Screw X 3 in.	⊟Product 1	⊟3	⊟$2.23	$4.45
		⊟Product 2	⊟12	⊟$0.16	$1.92
⊟01-000069-04	⊟#10 Screw X 10 in.	⊟Product 3	⊟10	⊟$0.25	$2.50
⊟01-000076-02	⊟#10 Screw X 3.75 in.	⊟Product 3	⊟12	⊟$0.19	$2.25
⊟01-000091-02	⊟#6 Screw X 1 in.	⊟Product 1	⊟10	⊟$0.17	$1.63
			⊟12	⊟$0.17	$2.01
⊟02-001132-02	⊟8 in Wheel	⊟Product 1	⊟4	⊟$1.50	$6.00
		⊟Product 2	⊟4	⊟$1.50	$6.00
⊟02-001132-03	⊟10 in Wheel	⊟Product 3	⊟4	⊟$2.50	$10.00
⊟03-010001-13	⊟6 in Rod	⊟Product 1	⊟2	⊟$2.23	$4.45
		⊟Product 3	⊟2	⊟$2.23	$4.45
⊟03-010001-15	⊟10 in Rod	⊟Product 2	⊟2	⊟$4.00	$8.00
⊟10-111554-04	⊟4 X 4 X 4 Enclosure	⊟Product 1	⊟1	⊟$45.00	$45.00
		⊟Product 3	⊟1	⊟$45.00	$45.00
⊟10-111554-08	⊟8 X 8 X 8 Enclosure	⊟Product 2	⊟1	⊟$82.00	$82.00

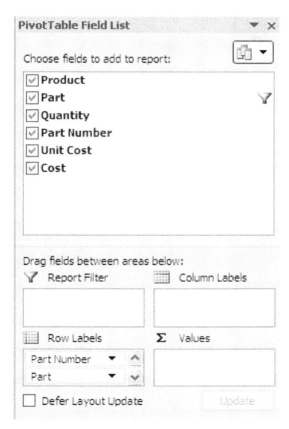

By filtering this list on one or more "Part Numbers" or "Parts", you can easily show which products a particular component or set of components goes into , including how many goes into each product and how much they cost.

Another way to present this is to drag "Product" into Drop Columns Fields Here area, and then drag "Part" into the "Drop Data Items Here" area:

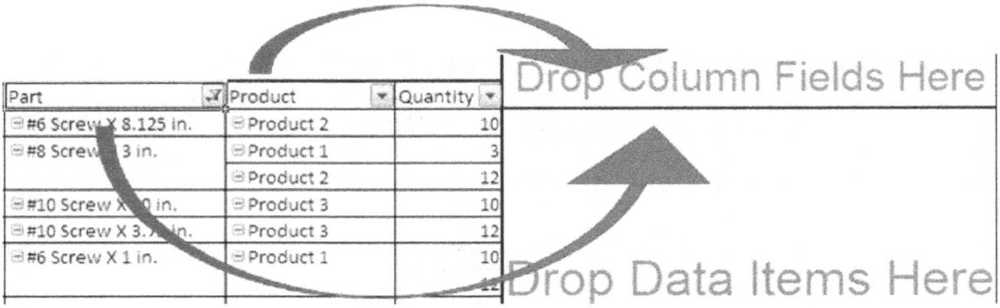

Part	Product	Quantity
#6 Screw X 8.125 in.	Product 2	10
#8 Screw 3 in.	Product 1	3
	Product 2	12
#10 Screw X 0 in.	Product 3	10
#10 Screw X 3.7 in.	Product 3	12
#6 Screw X 1 in.	Product 1	10

Drop Column Fields Here

Drop Data Items Here

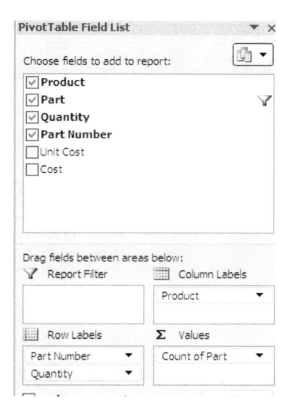

This results in a table which shows you by Product which ones contain certain parts and how many products contain each part:

Count of Part		Product			
Part Number	Quantity	Product 1	Product 2	Product 3	Grand Total
⊟ 01-000058-00	10		1		1
⊟ 01-000060-06	3	1			1
	12		1		1
⊟ 01-000069-04	10			1	1
⊟ 01-000076-02	12			1	1
⊟ 01-000091-02	10	1			1
	12	1			1
⊟ 02-001132-02	4	1	1		2
⊟ 02-001132-03	4			1	1
⊟ 03-010001-13	2	1		1	2
⊟ 03-010001-15	2		1		1
⊟ 10-111554-04	1	1		1	2
⊟ 10-111554-08	1		1		1
⊟ (blank)	(blank)	1	1	1	3
Grand Total		7	6	6	19

Any of these fields can be filtered to show only certain parts or certain components. From this chart it is easy to see which components appear in which products and which ones are used in only a few products, which ones are used in all products, etc.

How To Instantly Manage Training

Let's look at one more common example; training records.

TASK – <u>Provide A List of Who Has Completed What Training for all 8,000 Employees in your Company as Requested by the Compliance Auditor and Your Senior VP.</u>

<u>Situation</u>: You have compiled a list of the training courses completed for all 8,000 employees. Since each employee had taken multiple training courses over their careers, the list contains multiple entries for each of the 8,000 employees. The compliance auditor is concerned that certain employees performing key financial functions have not had specific training needed to comply with current regulations. If you company is found to be out of compliance, all of its products will be seized and sales to certain markets disallowed. There is a huge financial consequence to being found out of compliance so a quick and accurate answer to this question is critical. And this is all up to you!

How to do this? You could either use –

Option A – Review the list and highlight each identified critical training course and count up who has taken this one. Then type these results into a chart to make a report for management to provide the auditor. After you do this, they will probably have questions which require you to do more work (such as "what about this person", when did they complete the training", "did they complete the training the first time they took the course?"). This will force you to go back and start the chart over again, and again, and again…until you have figured out what they want. You may miss some information or make some mistakes along the way, so you will need to double-check your work, so allow more time for proofreading.

Or

Option B – Let The Computer Do The Work.

First start with the information you have. In this case, you have a long list of employees and line items indicating different training courses and statuses and completion dates:

EMP ID	Employee Name	Description	Completion Date	Status
0013775	CONNORS, STANLEY	Safety Training	2/4/2010	COMPLETED
0013775	CONNORS, STANLEY	Safety Training	2/4/2010	COMPLETED
0013775	CONNORS, STANLEY	Quality Training	5/13/2010	COMPLETED
0013775	CONNORS, STANLEY	Managing people	5/21/2010	COMPLETED
0013775	CONNORS, STANLEY	Information security policies	8/6/2010	COMPLETED
0013775	CONNORS, STANLEY	Fair trade regulations training	11/8/2010	COMPLETED
0013775	CONNORS, STANLEY	Safety Training	1/18/2011	COMPLETED
0013775	CONNORS, STANLEY	Information security policies	1/18/2011	COMPLETED
0013775	CONNORS, STANLEY	Safety Training	1/19/2011	COMPLETED
0013775	CONNORS, STANLEY	Safety Training	1/20/2011	COMPLETED
0013775	CONNORS, STANLEY	Project Management	3/14/2011	COMPLETED
0013775	CONNORS, STANLEY	Project Management	3/14/2011	COMPLETED
0013775	CONNORS, STANLEY	Fire Safety training	4/4/2011	COMPLETED
0013775	CONNORS, STANLEY	Business Continuity Planning (BCP) training	2/6/2012	COMPLETED

So, all the information you need to answer the auditor's questions is contained in the list, but it just needs to be organized and filtered.

Let's create a pivot table using this data and format it so that it shows employee name in the left hand column, followed by the training they have completed and the associated dates when they completed the training:

Count of Status				
Employee Name ▾	Description ▾	Status ▾	Completion Date ▾	Total
⊟ BROWN, JANE	⊟ Business Continuity Planning (E	⊟ COMPLETED	5/16/2013	1
			5/31/2013	1
			12/10/2011	1
		⊟ STARTED	5/31/2013	1
	⊟ Chemical Safety training	⊟ COMPLETED	6/22/2010	1
			7/8/2010	1
	⊟ Customer Service Training	⊟ COMPLETED	5/30/2013	1
	⊟ Design Process	⊟ COMPLETED	5/16/2013	1
	⊟ Environmental regulatons trair	⊟ COMPLETED	5/16/2013	1
	⊟ Harassment training	⊟ COMPLETED	5/16/2013	1
	⊟ Information security policies	⊟ COMPLETED	2/23/2011	1
			8/6/2010	1
	⊟ Managing people	⊟ COMPLETED	6/22/2010	1
	⊟ Purchasing training	⊟ COMPLETED	5/16/2013	1
			5/31/2013	1
	⊟ Quality Training	⊟ COMPLETED	5/31/2013	1
			6/22/2010	1
			12/10/2011	1
	⊟ Safety Training	⊟ COMPLETED	7/5/2010	1
			12/14/2011	1
	⊟ Sales training	⊟ COMPLETED	2/23/2011	1
	⊟ Testing Process	⊟ COMPLETED	5/16/2013	1
	⊟ Travel and entertainment spen	⊟ COMPLETED	5/23/2011	1
			7/22/2010	1
			7/6/2010	1
			7/7/2010	3
BROWN, JANE Total				28

In this case, the employee name is the high level field and the pivot table shows the relationships of the employee name to all the associated fields (training course, completion date, status). This would be a good format if the auditor was looking at a particular person and asked about what training they have completed. You could provide this table to your management and they would have the information they needed to be confident that the necessary training was competed by this individual.

But let's say the auditor shifts their focus and now asks "which employees have received Business Continuity Planning training"? So now they are looking for the high level field to be the training course description and the related fields to include the employee name and completion dates.

To do this, simply drag and "Description" field to the left-hand most column in the pivot table:

And then the pivot table will show the employees who have taken each training course. By filtering the Description column to show only "Business Continuity Planning", this will provide the information needed to answer this question of who has completed this training and when:

Count of Status

Description	Employee Name	EMP ID	Status	Completion Date
⊟Business Continuity Planning	⊟BROWN, JANE	⊟0071383	⊟COMPLETED	5/16/2013
				5/31/2013
				12/10/2011
			⊟STARTED	5/31/2013
	⊟CHEN, CHRISTOPHER	⊟0068456	⊟COMPLETED	2/13/2012
				5/20/2011
	⊟CONNORS, STANLEY	⊟0013775	⊟COMPLETED	2/6/2012
	⊟KOPP, ERIK	⊟0077158	⊟COMPLETED	2/21/2012
				5/10/2013
				8/30/2011
	⊟NORTH, DANIEL	⊟0079605	⊟COMPLETED	2/13/2012
	⊟SMITH, MICHAEL	⊟0071804	⊟COMPLETED	2/13/2012
				7/27/2011
	⊟WEST, JOHN	⊟0058261	⊟COMPLETED	2/6/2012
				8/4/2011
	⊟WILSON, SALLY	⊟0045309	⊟COMPLETED	11/21/201
				2/23/2012

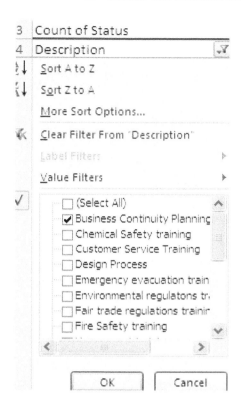

The list of examples can go on and on and also includes non-work projects (like evaluating a list of who is bringing what food and supplies to the class party, donations received by you church from different organizations, ordering history for you gardening club....). Once you have an understanding of how pivot tables work and what makes them so powerful, you will find many more uses for them which you never thought of before.

Any time you have a long list of items which need to be analyzed o presented in different ways, use pivot tables to automate your work. See how much time and effort you save. Answers to complex questions can be figured out in seconds.

Isn't this what computers were supposed to do for us – make our lives easier? Don't let computers take control of you and make you do more work, you can take control of them and make the computer do the work for you!

BONUS #2: Excel Macros That Send Outlook Emails

Life in business has become a constant juggling act of multiple do-it-yourself tasks. Getting projects completed correctly and on time involves your constant attention to making sure everyone does what they are supposed to and when they are supposed to do it. You cannot hand something off to someone else with the expectation that it will be done correctly or on time. This is because everyone else is just as crazy busy as you are and they face their own multi-tasking challenges as well.

This is where you need to rely on technology to help save you from dropping the balls you need to juggle.

One of the key business tools for managing projects today is email. Email enables instant communications to anywhere in the world and it provides a record of all communications (so you can prove you did what you were supposed to do). Thus email provides an ideal means of notifying people when they need to follow up on something.

For one or two projects, sending out email reminders to people works fine, but when you have 10 or more projects this manual process becomes unmanageable and mistakes happen (emails are not sent, emails sent to the wrong people, emails contain the wrong content). Email just become another lose end to manage.

There is software for managing projects and keeping track of tasks, but integrating this with email notification can be very complicated and result in extraneous cryptic notifications being sent out that are flagged as spam by the recipients.

Project plans can have several hundred tasks/subtasks and if you have multiple projects to work with you have several thousand tasks/subtasks to go through to find out which ones need attention and when. This can result in a lot of time spend and a lot of aggravation with little positive result.

What you need is a simple tool that automates what you would naturally do; make a list of what needs to be done, when it needs to be done and what you need from other people in order to get it done, and then start contacting those people to ask for their help. Very simple. It's just the volume and urgency of the tasks that gets in the way and makes this a tedious complicated chore to manage manually.

Fortunately, using common MS Office tools it is possible to create a simple customizable email notification system using MS Excel to create and send MS Outlook emails.

Using a simple list of tasks, due dates and email addresses in an Excel spreadsheet, you can add functionality using a simple VBA script which will create individualized emails and send them to the correct people (no mistakes or getting confused).

This book will walk you through step-by-step how to set up, customize and use a project email tracker spreadsheet to manage your email notifications. MS Excel 2007 and MS Outlook 2007 were used in these examples.

How To Manage Multiple Email Notifications Effectively

<u>Situation</u>: You are currently managing 6 project teams and sitting on 12 more as a key contributor. To accomplish your part for all of these requires key inputs from other people in other groups and locations. Your company is once again in a pinch and someone high up has promised senior management that all 18 key projects will be launched by the end of 3rd quarter and it is now August. So every task and every piece of all the puzzles is on the critical path. No one can be late with their deliverables by more than 1/2 day or launch deadlines will be missed. Nothing can slip – you cannot afford to forget about even one task. This requires constantly following up with many people and reminding them about what they need to do and when their part is due.

In the past each of these teams had project managers and these project managers had admins who kept on top of the task timelines and notified people when things were coming due. But over time, these resources were deemed to be "overhead" (not contributing directly to the bottom line) so their positions were eliminated, leaving you with the multiple responsibilities for managing the projects and doing the work.

So now, how can you keep on top on this?

Option A – You can make lists of what tasks you need to get done, what you need from whom and when you need it. And then notify these people every so often by creating emails and sending them out when you have time (and when you remember). This might work if you have a few projects to work on, but when the number of projects to manage at one time gets too high, you risk mistakes and items overlooked.

Or

Option B – Let The Computer Do The Work

Using a VBA (Visual Basic for Applications) enabled Excel

spreadsheet, you can create a simple To Do list which will track of your tasks and create individualized email notifications as needed based on the due dates and status of each task. With the click of one button, you can send out all of the needed email notifications using Outlook and keep a record of who you notified and when.

Here is an example of what this spreadsheet looks like. Go to www.erikkopponline.com/project-tracker for a copy of the excel spreadsheet used in this book. Password for the site and for the spreadsheet is "**Sunday**".

Today's Date:	Tuesday, July 23, 2013	Jim	Bcc email: (email1@domain1.com, email2@domain2.com.)					Password to Unprotect Worksheet: Sunday	CLICK To Send Notifications	
Project Name	Task	Assigned To Last Name	TO email: (email1@domain1.com, email2@domain2.com.)	cc email: (email1@domain1.com, email2@domain2.com.)	Due Date: (dd-mmm-yyyy or mm/dd/yyyy)	Complete (Yes/No)?	Due When? (system generated - do not alter)	Notification Message (system generated - do not alter)	Notification Sent (delete to remove history)
Implement new enterprise logistics system	Issue Project Plan	Kopp	ekpublications@comcast.net; erikkopp@comcast.net		Friday, July 19, 2013	Yes	Complete	Complete	• Thursday, July 18, 2013 - 12:23:24 PM • Thursday, July 18, 2013 - 12:22:25 PM • Thursday, July 18, 2013 - 1:30:17 PM • Thursday, July 18, 2013 - 1:29:21 PM
Create launch strategy	Submit market analysis trends report	Smith	ekpublications@comcast.net		Tuesday, July 16, 2013	Yes	Complete	Complete	• Thursday, July 18, 2013 - 1:37:11 PM
Develop new prototype	Validate design	Helen	ekpublications@comcast.net		Monday, July 15, 2013	No	Overdue - was due on Monday, July 15, 2013.	Your assigned task 'Validate design' for Project 'Develop new prototype' is Overdue - was due on Monday, July 15, 2013.	

Any cells highlighted in yellow need to be filled in for the spreadsheet to work.

Cells highlighted in blue are not to be modified. These are either headings (dark blue) or system generated information (light blue). These have been protected to prevent accidental modification or deletions (which can cause the script not to work). The password to unprotect the sheet is "Sunday", if you want to modify it. It would be a good idea first to save a backup copy of the spreadsheet with another name, just in case you need to get it back to where it was originally.

Using this spreadsheet, the following information is entered in:

- Project name
- Task
- Assigned to (First name, Last name)
- Email (To, cc, Bcc) – may be multiple, separated by ";"
- Due date
- Complete? (Yes/No)
- Name of person sending the email (From)

The spreadsheet then performs the following functions:

- Displays today's date
- Calculates status (Due When? / Over Due?) – based on due date and today's date.
- Creates notification message text "Your assigned task <task> s <Due When>"
- Sends email messages to indicated email addresses using Outlook, for tasks which are not complete.
- Records date/time that emails are sent.
- Saves the spreadsheet with the updated information.

For this example, there are 3 projects with tasks listed (but the spreadsheet can handle 500 and it can be modified to handle even more..). You can type in the project names in column A and the task names in columns B. One project may have multiple tasks. Here is how it looks in the example:

	A	B
1	**Today's Date:**	**Tuesday, July 23, 2013**
2	**Project Name**	**Task**
3	Implement new enteprise logistics system	Issue Project Plan
4	Implement new enteprise logistics system	Submit market analysis trends report
5	Develop new prototype	Validate design

In the next 4 columns, we enter in the people's names who we need to notify about these tasks and their email address (To) and anyone we wish to copy (cc – this is optional, may be left blank). Email addresses may be a single address per cell, or may be a list of addresses separated by a ";" (address1@email1.com;address2@email2.com;...addressn@emailn.com):

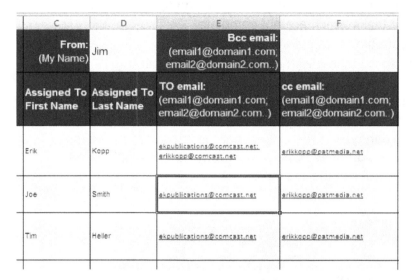

C	D	E	F
From: (My Name)	Jim	Bcc email: (email1@domain1.com; email2@domain2.com..)	
Assigned To First Name	Assigned To Last Name	TO email: (email1@domain1.com; email2@domain2.com..)	cc email: (email1@domain1.com; email2@domain2.com..)
Erik	Kopp	ekpublications@comcast.net; erikkopp@comcast.net	erikkopp@patmedia.net
Joe	Smith	ekpublications@comcast.net	erikkopp@patmedia.net
Tim	Heller	ekpublications@comcast.net	erikkopp@patmedia.net

The cell D1 as shown above contains the name of the person who is sending the email (the name that appears at the bottom of the email text i.e. Best regards, "Name").

Now in the next column, enter the due date for the task (this can be dd-mmm-yyyy [23-jul-2013] or mm/dd/yyyy [07/23/2013] either will work).

And in the next column indicate if the task is complete (pick list – Yes or No). If the task is complete, the spreadsheet will not send an email notification (no need to bug the person any longer).

G	H	
		Pa: Su
Due Date: (dd-mmm-yyyy or mm/dd/yyyy)	**Complete** (Yes/No)?	D (s no
Friday, July 26, 2013	No	Du
Tuesday, July 16, 2013	Yes	Co
Monday, July 15, 2013	No	Ov Jul
	Yes No	

The next 3 blue highlighted columns contain system generated information:

- Column I indicates the status (Due When – Complete, Overdue or Due in "X" days). This is a protected cell.

- Column J shows the notification message (email text) to be sent. This is set up using a concatenation function which merges the text "Your assigned task" with the name of the task and then the word "for" and then the name of the project and then "is" and then the text from Due Date. This is a protected cell. The function is :

=IF(B3="","",IF(H3="Yes","Complete","Your assigned task '"&B3&"' for Project '"&A3&"' is "&I3))

- Column K shows a running list of time and date when email notifications are sent. The list continues to grow each time you send a notifications, but you can delete the content s of this cell (it is not protected).

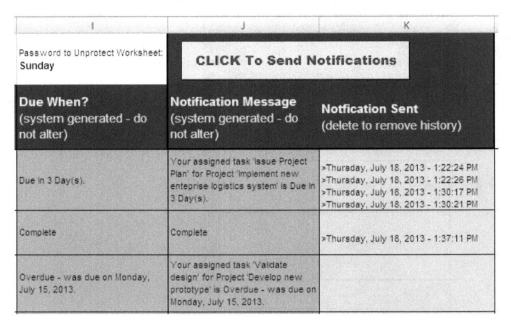

I	J	K
Password to Unprotect Worksheet: Sunday	**CLICK To Send Notifications**	
Due When? (system generated - do not alter)	**Notification Message** (system generated - do not alter)	**Notfication Sent** (delete to remove history)
Due In 3 Day(s).	Your assigned task 'Issue Project Plan' for Project 'Implement new enteprise logistics system' is Due In 3 Day(s).	>Thursday, July 18, 2013 - 1:22:24 PM >Thursday, July 18, 2013 - 1:22:26 PM >Thursday, July 18, 2013 - 1:30:17 PM >Thursday, July 18, 2013 - 1:30:21 PM
Complete	Complete	>Thursday, July 18, 2013 - 1:37:11 PM
Overdue - was due on Monday, July 15, 2013.	Your assigned task 'Validate design' for Project 'Develop new prototype' is Overdue - was due on Monday, July 15, 2013.	

And finally, the button is what you click to send the notifications once you have set up the spreadsheet.

This causes Outlook to send the emails from the notification message cells to the corresponding email addresses from you Outlook inbox. You must have Outlook running before you send the notifications. The messages will come from you Outlook email address.

The complete text of the email is:

Dear Tim,

Your assigned task 'Validate design' for Project 'Develop new prototype' is Overdue - was due on Monday, July 15, 2013.

Please provide a status update.

Regards,

Jim

The text "Please provide a status update" and "Regards" are part of the VBA code.

The spreadsheet shows the date and time this was sent:

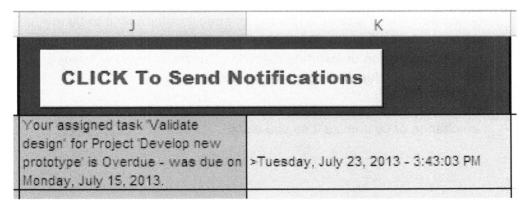

Notifications which are sent multiple times are shown as multiple entries in column K (one line for each time sent) until the cell is cleared.

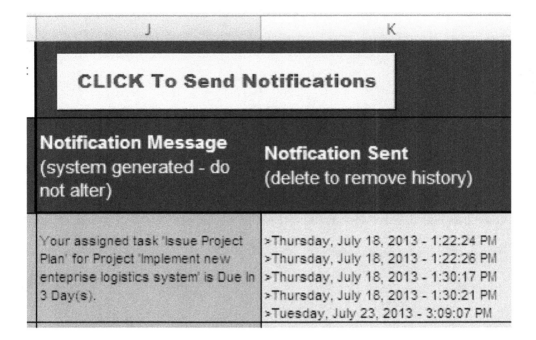

If the spreadsheet works for you this way, please feel free to use it just as it is. If you would like to change it, please read on we will cover this in the next chapters.

Please note that the code is looking for specific information to be in specific cells, so any changes to the spreadsheet format or layout (i.e. moving information or inserting/deleting columns or rows) will cause the code to stop functioning as it was designed.

In the next chapters we will get into how the code works so that you can change or customize it as you want.

Setting Up A Project Email Tracker in Excel

The first thing you need to do is to make sure Excel is set up to display the "Developer" tool bar.

To do this – first click the Office button:

Then click "Excel Options":

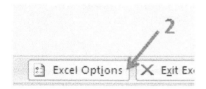

In the Excel Option window, make sure "Show Developer tab in the Ribbon" is checked:

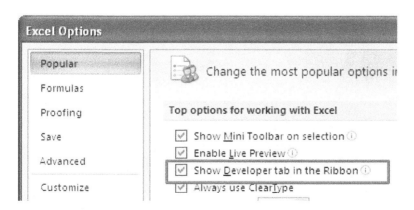

Developer will then appear as a tab:

Then save the spreadsheet as an "Excel Macro-Enabled Workbook":

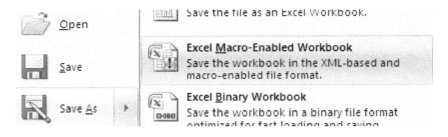

This enables the VBA scripts to be functional and it saves the spreadsheet with the extension ".xlsm".

You can then go to the Developer tab and click the "Macros" button:

This will open up the Macro window:

Then type a name for the new script into the Macro name box, then click "Create":

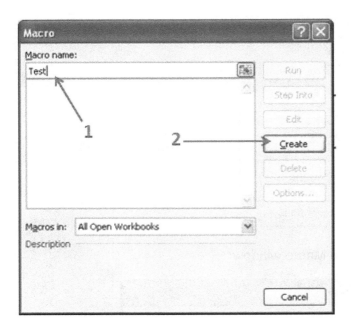

This launches the Visual Basic (VBA) code window:

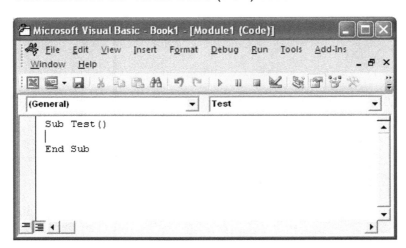

You can now either type in the VBA code you need to create and send emails, or you can cut and paste the code into the editor window.

Since this isn't supposed to be a technical manual about

programming, I would recommend you go to www.erikkopponline.com/project-tracker for a copy of the excel spreadsheet used in this book. Password for the site and for the spreadsheet is "**Sunday**".

This is a fully functional macro enabled spreadsheet which enables you to create and send multiple Outlook emails in an automated manner at the click of one button. Feel free to use this as-is or modify it as needed.

Instructions for using the spreadsheet are found in **Chapter 4**

An explanation of how the spreadsheet works are found in **Chapter 3**. This detail is provided so you can understand how to modify it if you want to.

How The Excel Project Email Tracker Works

Go to www.erikkopponline.com/project-tracker for a copy of the excel spreadsheet used in this book. Password for the site and for the spreadsheet is "**Sunday**".

So how does this spreadsheet work?

I promise that this is not a technical manual with boring code description, but I want to share with you a few key technical points because it will allow you to customize this spreadsheet to work the way you want it to.

The email tracker spreadsheet requires the use of a VBA script to provide the functionality needed to send emails using Outlook. VBA (Visual Basic for Applications) is a programming language supported by MS Office applications (such as Word, Excel and Outlook) for automating functions. Excel has many predefined formulas that provide a lot of functionality, but there are none with are capable of sending email. Therefore VBA is a must have for being able to accomplish the task of automating the sending of emails from an Excel spreadsheet.

We are not going to complete a course in programming here - I promise, but I do want to give you enough information to be able to understand how to change this script to make it do exactly what you want it to do.

Here is the code in its entirety (zoom in and take a look):

```
VBA code.txt - Notepad
File Edit Format View Help
Sub Project_Notification()
Dim Email_Subject, Email_From, Email_To, Email_Cc, Email_Bcc, Email_Message As
String
Dim Mail_object, Mail_send As Variant
For r = 3 To 500
If Sheets("Project Tracker").cells(r, 10) = "complete" Then
GoTo Skip
End If
If Sheets("Project Tracker").cells(r, 2) = "" Then
GoTo Skip
End If
If Sheets("Project Tracker").cells(r, 1) = "" Then
Exit For
End If
Email_Subject = Sheets("Project Tracker").cells(r, 1) & " Status Update."
Email_To = Sheets("Project Tracker").cells(r, 5)
Email_Cc = Sheets("Project Tracker").cells(r, 6)
Email_Bcc = Sheets("Project Tracker").cells(1, 6)
Email_Message = "Dear " & Sheets("Project Tracker").cells(r, 3) & "," & Chr(10) &
Chr(10) & Sheets("Project Tracker").cells(r, 10) & Chr(10) & Chr(10) & "Please
provide a status update." & Chr(10) & Chr(10) & "Regards," & Chr(10) & Chr(10) &
Sheets("Project Tracker").cells(1, 4)
On Error GoTo debugs
Set Mail_object = CreateObject("Outlook.Application")
Set Mail_send = Mail_object.CreateItem(0)
With Mail_send
.Subject = Email_Subject
.To = Email_To
.cc = Email_Cc
.BCC = Email_Bcc
.Body = Email_Message
.send
Worksheets("Project Tracker").cells(r, 11).value = cells(r, 11).value & Chr(10) &
">" & Format(Sheets("Project Tracker").cells(1, 7), "long date") & " - " &
Format(Sheets("Project Tracker").cells(1, 7), "long time")
Rows(r).EntireRow.AutoFit
Skip:
End With
debugs:
If Err.Description <> "" Then MsgBox Err.Description
Next r
Thisworkbook.Save
End Sub
```

The commands : "Set Mail_Object =
CreateObject("Outlook.Application")" and "Set Mail_Send =
Mail_Object.CreateItem(0)" enable Excel to send email using MS
Outlook.

The content of the email is defined by the commands:

With Mail_Send (initiates the function)
.Subject = Email_Subject (populates email subject)
.To = Email_To (populates email To address)
.cc = Email_Cc (populates email cc address)
.BCC = Email_Bcc (populates email Bcc address)
.Body = Email_Message (populates email message text)
.send (sends email from Outlook)

The script is designed to specifically look for a worksheet called Project Tracker using the command "Sheets("Project Tracker")". Therefore if the name of the worksheet is changed, the script command must also be changed or will not find the information it is looking for:

The script also includes a loop function which causes the commands to be run multiple times while it goes down the rows in the spreadsheet searching for information to populate into the emails. The loop starts at "3" and counts by 1 until it reaches "500" or until it encounters and exception. We'll discuss that it a minute:

```
Sub Project_Notification()
Dim Email_Subject, Email_Fr
String
Dim Mail_Object, Mail_Send
For r = 3 To 500
If Sheets("Project Tracker'
GoTo Skip
End If
If Sheets("Project Tracker'
GoTo Skip
End If
If Sheets("Project Tracker'
Exit For
End If
Email_Subject = Sheets("Pro
Email_To = Sheets("Project
Email_Cc = Sheets("Project
Email_Bcc = Sheets("Project
Email_Message = "Dear " & S
Chr(10) & Sheets("Project
provide a status update." &
Sheets("Project Tracker").C
On Error GoTo debugs
Set Mail_Object = Createob
Set Mail_Send = Mail_Objci
With Mail_Send
.Subject = Email_Subject
.To = Email_To
.CC = Email_Cc
.BCC = Email_Bcc
.Body = Email_Message
.send
Worksheets("Project Tracker
Tracker").Cells(1, 7), "  or
Tracker").Cells(1, 7), "  or
Skip:
End With
debugs:
If Err.Description <> ""  Th
Next r
ThisWorkbook.Save
End Sub
```

The significance of "3" is that this is the first row in the spreadsheet where the data appears and "500" is the last. but you could easily change this now that you understand how the script works.

Within the functions of the script the counter variable "r" is used to designate the row number the script is pointing at when it looks for data.

As the loop variable "r" counts from 3 to 500, the functions access various cells in the spreadsheet using the command "Cells(r, 5)" where "r" is the row number (which keeps getting larger by one each time the loop counts up.

The second number in the Cells function is the column number, where column "A" is "1", "B" is "2"..."Z" is 26"..etc.

A mapping of the row,column numbers is shown below:

	A	B	C	D	E	F	G	H	I	J	K
1	1,1	1,2	1,3	1,4	1,5	1,6	1,7	1,8	1,9	1,10	
2	2,1	2,2	2,3	2,4	2,5	2,6	2,7	2,8	2,9	2,10	
3	3,1	3,2	3,3	3,4	3,5	3,6	3,7	3,8	3,9	3,10	
4	4,1	4,2	4,3	4,4	4,5	4,6	4,7	4,8	4,9	4,10	
5	5,1	5,2	5,3	5,4	5,5	5,6	5,7	5,8	5,9	5,10	
6	6,1	6,2	6,3	6,4	6,5	6,6	6,7	6,8	6,9	6,10	
7	7,1	7,2	7,3	7,4	7,5	7,6	7,7	7,8	7,9	7,10	
8	8,1	8,2	8,3	8,4	8,5	8,6	8,7	8,8	8,9	8,10	
9	9,1	9,2	9,3	9,4	9,5	9,6	9,7	9,8	9,9	9,10	
10	10,1	10,2	10,3	10,4	10,5	10,6	10,7	10,8	10,9	10,10	
11											
12											
13											

CELLS (row,column)

So, if you wanted to look in Cell "G1" in the spreadsheet, the command to point to this would be "Cells(7,1)". Since the row in the script is using the "r" loop variable, the script will look in row 3, then row 4, then row 5…all the way to row 500 and then it will stop. If you need to make the list longer, you can revise the script to change this line "For r = 3 To 500" to specify the ending line. For example, if you wanted it to manage a list of 1,500 items, you could change this to "For r = 3 To 1503".

The column numbers are fixed in the VBA code and are designed to work with the spreadsheet as it is currently set up (i.e. Due Date is in column "G" or Column "7", etc.). This VBA command is a fixed lookup and does not move as the spreadsheet is modified. This is why it is important not to modify the spreadsheet unless you will also modify the script to accommodate this.

If you were to insert a column before "G" or move the Due Date to another column or do anything that causes the Due Date not to be in column "G", then the script would still look in column "G" and use whatever information it found there. This may cause it to return results that do not make sense, or it may just crash or return an error.

So if you need to move any columns, make sure you modify the "Cells" commands accordingly. Let's say you inserted a new column into the spreadsheet after column "F" that caused the Due Date to move to column "H", and every column after moves over by one as well ("H" becomes "I", "I" becomes "J", etc.). In the VBA code, you must then find every Cells command which specifies a column number of "7" or greater and add "1" to it so that the script can still find the information it is looking for (i.e. change "Cells(r,7)" to "Cells(r,8)" and change "Cells(r,8)" to "Cells(r,9)"…etc.).

As noted earlier, there are exceptions which cause the script to stop. Even though the script may be capable of executing 500 emails, or more if you modify it, you do not always want to send this many. Reasons for not sending an email for each line in the spreadsheet include:

- There are less than 500 tasks in the spreadsheet
- Some tasks are already complete, so there is no need for further notification.

To capture these in the script, there are some IF commands which look at specific information in the spreadsheet.

Going back to the 2 requirements noted above:

1. If there are less than 500 tasks. How would we know this? Either the cell containing the Project name" or "Task name would be blank" because we never entered any information here or we the entries were deleted. Let's say if the Task Name is blank but there is a project name, then skip this task and move on to the next row. But if there is no project name, then end the script because we have reached the end of the list.

IMPORTANT NOTE: If there are any blank projects within the list, the script will stop at the first blank project and not continue on, so do not leave any blank project entries within the list.

The code to check for this is

"If Sheets("Project Tracker").Cells(r, 2) = "" Then
GoTo Skip
End If"

[if the cell for Task name (column "2" or "B") is blank, then Skip* the row and continue the loop with the next row]

*The Skip command appears at the bottom of the script before the end of the loop but after all the email commands, so the script will not send any emails for these rows where Task name is blank:

"**Skip**:
End With
debugs:
If Err.Description <> "" Then MsgBox Err.Description
Next r"

And for the second condition:

"If Sheets("Project Tracker").Cells(r, 1) = "" Then
Exit For
End If"

[if the Project Name is blank (column "1" or "A") then stop the loop counter and exit – the script presumes we have reached the end of the list]

2. If tasks are not blank but are already complete, do not send an email notification. How do we know this? The cells in column "H" are set to either "Yes" or "No" to indicate if the tasks are complete or not.

The code to check for this is:

"If Sheets("Project Tracker").Cells(r, 10) = "Complete" Then
GoTo Skip
End If"

[if the cell for complete status (column "J" or "10") indicates the task is complete, then Skip* the row and continue the loop with the next row]

The commands in the script that actually compose and send the email are:

"Email_Subject = Sheets("Project Tracker").Cells(r, 1) & " Status Update."
Email_To = Sheets("Project Tracker").Cells(r, 5)
Email_Cc = Sheets("Project Tracker").Cells(r, 6)
Email_Bcc = Sheets("Project Tracker").Cells(1, 6)
Email_Message = "Dear " & Sheets("Project Tracker").Cells(r, 3) & ","
& Chr(10) & Chr(10) & Sheets("Project Tracker").Cells(r, 10) &
Chr(10) & Chr(10) & "Please provide a status update." & Chr(10) &
Chr(10) & "Regards," & Chr(10) & Chr(10) & Sheets("Project
Tracker").Cells(1, 4)"

The within the loop function so using the Cells command, an email is sent for each row of information in the spreadsheet until the loop ends (either counts yup to 500 or encounters one of the exceptions we discussed above).

So how does this work?

"Email_Subject = Sheets("Project Tracker").Cells(r, 1) & " Status

Update."

[reads the information in the cells in column "A" or "1" <project name> and adds the text "Status Update". This string "<project name> Status Update" becomes the Subject in the email. This is repeated for each row.]

"Email_To = Sheets("Project Tracker").Cells(r, 5)"

[takes the contents of the cells in column "5" or "E" and populates the "To" address in the emails. This is repeated for each row.]

"Email_Cc = Sheets("Project Tracker").Cells(r, 6)"

[takes the contents of the cells in column "6" or "F" and populates the "cc" address in the emails. This is repeated for each row.]

"Email_Bcc = Sheets("Project Tracker").Cells(1, 6)"

[takes the contents of the cell "F1" in row "1" / column "6" and populates the "Bcc" address in the emails. This statement indicates this is a fixed cell in the spreadsheet and the same address is used as "Bcc" for all emails.]

"Email_Message = "Dear " & Sheets("Project Tracker").Cells(r, 3) & "," & Chr(10) & Chr(10) & Sheets("Project Tracker").Cells(r, 10) & Chr(10) & Chr(10) & "Please provide a status update." & Chr(10) & Chr(10) & "Regards," & Chr(10) & Chr(10) & Sheets("Project Tracker").Cells(1, 4)"

[this one looks complicated so let's break it down. Basically this is the command that sends the email message. The message includes the text "Dear" and then the first name of the person as stated in the cells in column "C" or "3" in the spreadsheet (Cells(r, 3)), then there are 2 carriage returns (Chr(10P) adds a blank line, like hitting the enter key), and then the text from the spreadsheet in column "J" or "10" (Cells(r, 10) – Notification message) and then 2 more carriage returns followed by the text "Please provide a status update". Finally, there are 2 more carriage returns and then the text "Regards," followed by 2 more carriage returns and then finally the name of the person sending the message as stated in the spreadsheet in cell "D1" or "Cells(1,4)" – this is set to look at a fixed cell so the same name will appear at the end of all the messages. Except for "Bcc" address and the name at the end, all of the other content of the message will be unique to what is in each row of the spreadsheet. Any Cells commands which specify "r" as the row (rather than a number) will vary as they read each row in the spreadsheet.]

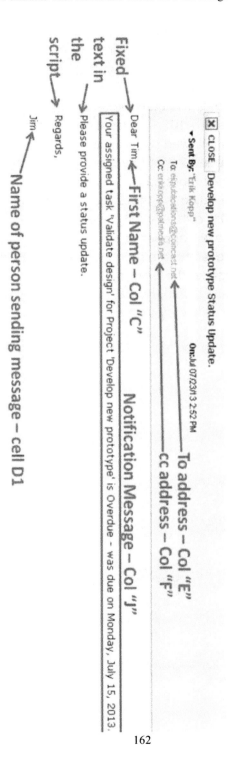

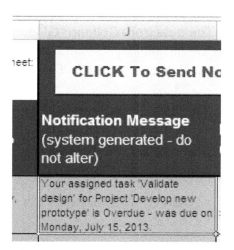

The message "Your assigned task 'Validate design' for Project 'Develop new prototype' is Overdue - was due on Monday, July 15, 2013." is created within the spreadsheet using standard Excel formulas:

"=IF(B5="","",IF(H5="Yes","Complete","Your assigned task '"&B5&"' for Project '"&A5&"' is "&I5))"

This functionality looks at the contents of the cells in column "H" to see if you have selected "Yes" for complete. If yes, then the result in column "J" is "Complete" and the script skips over this task ard does not send any emails. If no, then the text "Your assigned task" plus the task name from column "B" plus the text "for project" plus the project name from column "A" plus "is" plus the text from column "I" due when.

In column "I" there are also standard Excel formulas which calculate the due date status by comparing the due date entered in column "G" with the current system date in cell "B1"*. The result can be:

- "Due in X days" if due date is greater than current date.
- "Due NOW" if due date is equal to current date.

- "Overdue, was due on <Due Date – Col "G">" if due date is less than current date. The date from Column "G" is formatted to display the date in the format Day, Month, Day, Year ("dddd, mmmm dd, yyyy" ex: Tuesday, July 23, 2013).

This is accomplished by using the formula:

"=IF(H5="Yes","Complete",IF(B5="","",IF(G5-$B$1>0,"Due In "&G5-$B$1&" Day(s).",IF(G5-$B$1=0,"Due NOW.","Overdue - was due on "&TEXT(G5,"[$-F800]dddd, mmmm dd, yyyy")&"."))))"

*Cell B1 contains the Excel formula "=TODAY()" which returns the current system date.

There is one more thing the script does, it writes the date and time that it sends the emails into column ""K":

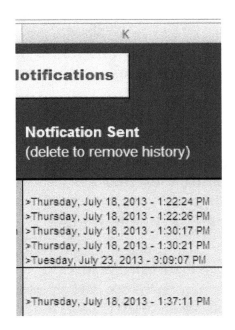

This is accomplished using the commands in the script:

"Worksheets("Project Tracker").Cells(r, 11).Value = Cells(r, 11).Value & Chr(10) & ">" & Format(Sheets("Project Tracker").Cells(1, 7), "long date") & " - " & Format(Sheets("Project

Tracker").Cells(1, 7), "long time")"

This command writes text into the cells in column "K" or "11" [Worksheets("Project Tracker").Cells(r, 11).Value =] which are equal to the date in cell "G1"* or Cells(1,7)* formatted in the long date format (ex: Thursday, July 18, 2013) followed by a "-" and then the time in cell "G1"* or Cells(1,7)* formatted in the long time format (ex: 1:37:11 PM).

*Cell G1 contains the Excel formula "=NOW()" which returns the current system date and time. This is shaded over in the spreadsheet so it is not visible.

Finally, the script does some cleanup and housekeeping tasks before it quits. These include:

- Resizing the rows to fit the information - using the command "Rows(r).EntireRow.AutoFit". This is important as the time/date entries in column "K" grow.

- Notifying the user of any errors using the command "debugs: If Err.Description <> "" Then MsgBox Err.Description"

- Saving the worksheet using the command "ThisWorkbook.Save". This is important or else the information in Column "K" will be lost.

With this information, you have the knowledge you need if you choose to make changes/modification to the project email tracker spreadsheet to better meet your needs.

Quick Reference Guide To Using And Modifying The Excel Email Tracker Spreadsheet

To use the Excel Email Tracker Spreadsheet:

- Obtain a copy of the spreadsheet from www.erikkopponline.com/project-tracker

- Open the spreadsheet in Excel. Please be sure to allow Macros to run. (This may require changing the Macro Settings in the Trust Center)

o Click the MS Office button and then select Excel Options)

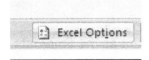

o Select Trust Center

o Click the Trust Center Settings button

o Click the circle by "Disable all macros with notification. This will not run the macro automatically but will notify you first if you want to run it.

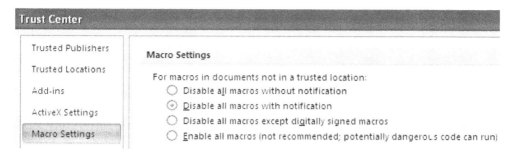

o Make sure to enable the content when you get the alert.

o Click the Options button, and then select "Enable this content" if you want the macro to run.

o Another option is to place the Excel spreadsheet into a "trusted location". Files located in a trusted location will be allowed to run.

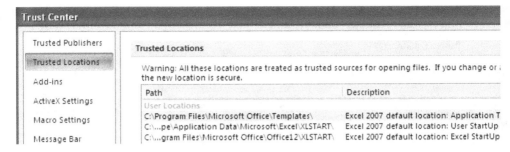

- Once the spreadsheet is open, fill in the appropriate information in the yellow highlighted cells.

- Select complete "Yes" or "No" as appropriate for each task.

- Click the "Click To Send Notifications" button.

- If Excel returns a message such as shown below, click "Ok". This allows the spreadsheet to be saved.

- The spreadsheet can be closed. It has already been saved with the notification dates/times.

To Unprotect the spreadsheet:

- Under the Review tab, click the "Unprotect Sheet" button

- Then enter the password "**Sunday**".

- Then click "OK".

To Protect the spreadsheet:

- Under the Review tab, click the "Protect Sheet" button

- Then select what you want the users to be able to do in the "Protect Sheet" window. This has been set up as shown below to give users the access they need for the spreadsheet to run and some modifications to be made that will not negatively impact the script.

- Then enter in a password and click "OK".

<u>To access the VBA code</u>:

- Under the Developer tab, click the "Visual Basic" button:

- This launches the Visual basic window showing the code.

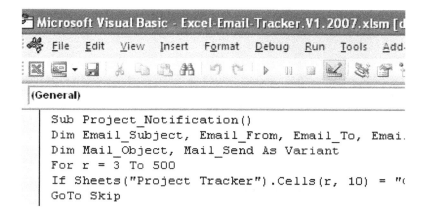

```
Microsoft Visual Basic - Excel-Email-Tracker.V1.2007.xlsm [d

  File   Edit   View   Insert   Format   Debug   Run   Tools   Add.

(General)

  Sub Project_Notification()
  Dim Email_Subject, Email_From, Email_To, Emai.
  Dim Mail_Object, Mail_Send As Variant
  For r = 3 To 500
  If Sheets("Project Tracker").Cells(r, 10) = "(
  GoTo Skip
```

- From this window you can view and modify the code as needed.

- When modifications are complete, save the code using the save button and click "Debug" to test the code and find any errors.

To change the email message:

- Unprotect the spreadsheet as described above.

- Modify the formulas in the spreadsheet used to create the message (Column "J" and Column "I"). You will be able to see the message in the spreadsheet in Column "J".

- Open the Visual Basic window as described above.

- Modify the VBA command "mail_Message = "Dear " & Sheets("Project Tracker").Cells(r, 3) & "," & Chr(10) & Chr(10) & Sheets("Project Tracker").Cells(r, 10) & Chr(10) & Chr(10) & "Please provide a status update." & Chr(10) & Chr(10) & "Regards," & Chr(10) & Chr(10) & Sheets("Project Tracker").Cells(1, 4)".

You will need to send out a test email in order to see the result of this change.

- Protect the sheet as described above.

The Mission Of This Book

As organizations continue to restructure and become more lean than ever, many of us find ourselves today with more and more work to do since there are less and less people left to do it. When my parents were in the work force, if you needed a report written or a presentation put together you could ask your department secretary (later renamed the "admin") or you could go to the graphics department to help you out. Today the expectation is that you will do all of this work yourself. In addition, as people leave organizations the expectation is that business continues on as usual with no interruptions; which means their work gets added onto yours.

The first reaction to this is to try to step up by putting in more hours and work harder than ever to hold on to what you have and be grateful you are a survivor. This may work temporarily, until you either get burned out or run into a clash with your other life (spouse, kids, family, church, health). The problem here is that simply doing more of what you did before is not going to work out in the long term. If the answer is simply more hours, it will not be long before these hours are transferred to someone somewhere else in the world where labor costs are much lower. The real answer for proving your value to our organization and keeping your sanity is to find ways to do things differently such that you can get the most work done in the least amount of time.

With the tools you have uncovered in this book, you will have unlocked the power to accomplish additional tasks in a fraction of the time it would take you using the manual means.